ALIF BAA

INTRODUCTION TO ARABIC LETTERS AND SOUNDS

ألف باء

مدخل الى حروف العربية وأصواتها

The production of this textbook and all accompanying audio and video tapes was supported by a grant from the National Endowment for the Humanities, an independent federal agency.

ALIF BAA

INTRODUCTION TO ARABIC LETTERS AND SOUNDS

ألف باء

مدخل الى حروف العربية وأصواتها

Kristen Brustad *Mahmoud Al-Batal* *Abbas Al-Tonsi*

كرستن بروستاد محمود البطل عباس التونسي

Georgetown University Press/Washington D.C.

Georgetown University Press, Washington, D.C.

Printed in the United States of America
10 9 8 7 6 5 4 3 1995
THIS VOLUME IS PRINTED ON ACID-FREE OFFSET BOOK PAPER

Library of Congress Cataloging-in-Publication Data

Brustad, Kristen.
Alif baa : introduction to Arabic letters and sounds / Kristen Brustad, Mahmoud Al-Batal, Abbas Al-Tonsi.
p. cm.
1. Arabic language--Writing. 2. Arabic language--Alphabet.
I. Al-Batal, Mahmoud. II. Tūnisī, ᶜAbbās. III. Title.
PJ6123.A54 1995
492' .78--dc20
ISBN 0-87840-292-6 (paper) 95-6981

TABLE OF CONTENTS

Unit Three: الوحدة الثالثة

Unit Four: الوحدة الرابعة

Unit Five: الوحدة الخامسة

Unit Nine: الوحدة التاسعة

Unit Ten: الوحدة العاشرة

PREFACE

To the Student

Ahlan wa Sahlan! Welcome to Arabic! This textbook, *Alif Baa*, represents the first in a series of textbooks aimed at teaching Arabic to English-speaking students, followed by *Al-Kitaab fii Ta^callum al-^cArabiyya I & II.*

The present book aims to help you learn to produce Arabic sounds and write its letters, and to introduce to you a number of greetings, common phrases, and basic vocabulary, as well as aspects of Arab culture. The book is accompanied by a set of audio tapes for you to use outside of class and a video tape that you will watch in class with your teacher.

The book consists of an introduction, ten units, an appendix and an English-Arabic Glossary. The introduction provides a brief overview of some special characteristics of Arabic, and the ten units present the alphabet in groups following the modern Arabic order, with the exception that all of the long vowels are presented in the first unit. In describing the sounds, we have avoided technical descriptions, opting instead for a more practical approach involving tips and exercises that focus on the points of articulation of the sounds. Following the description of each sound, we have provided a brief explanation of the writing of the corresponding letter. Each unit contains a number of recorded listening exercises and drills on reading, writing, connecting letters, and dictation. We have used only meaningful words in these exercises, because word structure in Arabic is based on consonant-vowel patterns, and listening to a large number of words, even if you do not know their meaning, will help you begin internalizing these patterns and facilitate learning vocabulary. We have also included in this book examples of authentic or "real-life" Arabic from newspapers, books, and magazines. Finally, we have included short cultural notes explaining aspects of the situations that you will see on the accompanying video tape. The appendix provides the texts of all the dialogues on the video tape, and the glossary includes all the vocabulary items introduced in the book.

We believe that it is crucial for you to learn to recognize and produce Arabic sounds accurately from the outset, for several reasons. First, you must learn to pronounce Arabic correctly in order to communicate effectively with Arabic speakers. Arabic has its own unique beauty, and the extent to which you learn the sounds correctly reflects, among other things, the degree of respect you have for the language and its speakers. Second, Arabic sounds are not very difficult. Many non-native speakers have learned to pronounce Arabic sounds accurately, and there is no reason why you should not expect to do so as well. Third, it is important to learn the sounds correctly now when you have the time and energy to concentrate on them; later you will be concentrating on other aspects of the language, such as vocabulary and grammar. Fourth, the structure of the Arabic language is such that being able to recognize sounds when you hear them will greatly enhance your ability to learn, understand, and remember vocabulary. Fifth, Arabic is largely phonetic, which means that if you learn the sounds correctly now, you will not suffer from spelling headaches. Finally, we do not agree with the commonly held assumption that Arabic is too difficult for non-native speakers to learn: all languages require a certain amount of exposure, time, and effort, and the ability to learn a foreign language is directly related to both the desire to do so and the belief that you can.

Tips for Using This Book:

1. **Prepare for active participation in class.** Listen to the tapes and prepare the lesson assigned beforehand, so that you will be ready to read and write. Class time should be spent practicing, not listening to lectures.

2. **Once is not enough.** Whether you are pronouncing new sounds, writing new letters, or studying vocabulary, you should repeat the activity as many times as you can. Repeat until you can produce a sound or write a letter easily. Remember that you are training your brain and your muscles to do new things, and this takes practice. Listen to the tapes as many times as you can, and go back over items that you missed on the homework. Although most of your studies are visually oriented, you learned your native language mainly through hearing and listening, and not through reading and writing. Rediscover your native ability to learn through listening by devoting as much time as you can while working through this book to the listening and dictation exercises.

3. **Study out loud.** The only way to train your brain and your mouth to speak this language is by doing—thinking about it is not enough!

4. **Study in groups.** You are much more likely to study **actively** when you study with others. Good group activities include quizzing and dictating to each other, and making up sentences and dialogues.

5. **Review constantly.** Set aside part of your study time each day to go over old material and practice sounds and letters you learned previously. This investment will pay off in improved accuracy in listening, speaking, reading and writing.

6. **Expect to feel tired occasionally.** Being tired is a good sign—it means that you are concentrating, and that you are training your muscles to produce new sounds correctly. Remember that you will soon be able to do easily things that tire you at first.

We wish you a successful and enjoyable learning experience!

To the Teacher

The philosophy behind this textbook represents a departure from that of previous alphabet textbooks in several ways. First, it is our belief that everyone can produce Arabic sounds accurately, and that it is necessary to encourage and expect accuracy from the outset. Not only is this the only opportunity you and the students will have to focus all of your attention on the phonetic aspects of Arabic, it is also better to form good habits from the start. Second, we believe that all language skills are important, and that they reinforce each other. The ability to hear the difference between, for example, ك and ق , is a necessary prelude to being able to produce them, and the ability to do both will aid in mastering Arabic morphology, in writing, and in retaining vocabulary. Third, we believe that Arabic is one language, albeit one rich in varieties, and that each variety embraces its own level or part of the culture. In order to understand the language and the culture, students need to learn both formal and spoken varieties. It is the goal of this textbook series to provide a framework for introducing students to both varieties while focusing on the formal; the extent to which you emphasize each variety will depend on your program and the needs of your students. We have found through experience that this approach does not confuse students, as long as spoken variants are introduced as vocabulary items and expressions. On the contrary, it adds to their pool of vocabulary, and, more importantly, gives them the tools they need to begin communicating with native speakers they might meet or know in their immediate environment, who will not speak to them in formal Arabic.

The material in this textbook can be covered in twenty to twenty-five contact hours, depending on the amount of time devoted to the various activities, and assuming that the student will devote one to two hours a night to doing the drills. The book is designed so that the student can do much of his or her learning outside of class. Class time should be spent on practice rather than explanations. We believe that it is crucial for the students to learn the sounds correctly from the outset. In order to help them do so, spend as much class time as possible on activities involving listening, dictation, and reading aloud. Our approach stresses dictation because we believe that the mastery of sounds and the ability to relate sounds and writing must be developed early. Repeat sounds and words many times over, and have students repeat as a group to take the pressure off individual performance. It takes several repetitions of a new or unfamiliar sound in order to identify it, and several more to be able to produce it.

The accompanying video tape contains some basic dialogues that were filmed in Egypt in the Cairene dialect. Our decision to use colloquial Arabic was a natural consequence of our desire to include a cultural component in these materials, and to use language forms appropriate to that component. Many culturally important expressions belong to the colloquial register, and introducing the students to them as they naturally occur helps them to feel that they are learning to communicate with Arabs. We decided to use the dialect of Cairo in this first edition of the materials because it is the most widely understood among Arabic speakers. However, it is not our desire to impose the teaching of the Egyptian dialect on anyone; if your own dialect differs, we encourage you to teach your students the forms with which you are comfortable. (We do not believe you will find the differences to be very great.)

We hope that you will make use of the accompanying video tape not only for its linguistic value but also for its visual and cultural content. You will need to use the tape in class in order to explain the content. We have distributed the eighteen dialogues over the first nine units. While we have included short cultural notes in the book meant to accompany the video scenes, we have not provided detailed lesson plans in order to give you the flexibility to proceed as you wish and focus on the aspects you deem important. Use the tape and cultural notes as starting points, encourage questions and discussion, and expand as you wish. We suggest that you have the students listen to each dialogue several times as follows: (1) Before explaining anything, have them watch for general content, then discuss, and see what they understood. (2) Have them watch again, as many times as necessary, to listen for individual words or expressions, followed by discussion and explanation of what they heard. (3) Have them watch a final time, after they have understood *what* is said, to focus on *how* it is said. After that, the students should be ready to try out the expressions themselves, so let them make up their own situations and act them out. Your own contribution will be vital to the success of these materials.

Do not worry about writing out the dialogues. It is good training for the students to develop confidence in their aural and oral skills at this stage, and they need to be encouraged to rely on their "phonographic" rather than their "photographic" memory. Everybody has natural aural and oral language learning skills, because nobody learned their native language through reading. As the students master the alphabet, they will be able to study from the transcribed texts in the appendix.

Of course, no textbook can take the place of a good teacher. It is our hope that these materials will help you to enrich your classroom and make learning Arabic an enjoyable experience for your students.

ACKNOWLEDGMENTS

We would like to express our deep gratitude to all the institutions and individuals who made the production of this book possible. The National Endowment for the Humanities provided the funding for the project through a grant to the School of Arabic at Middlebury College. Middlebury College provided matching funds and staff support. The Egyptian Union for Television and Radio graciously granted permission for us to use a number of its video materials and provided us with copies of a number of its programs.

We are grateful to the many people who have helped with different phases of the project. To mention just a few, Mary Nachtrieb and Hicham Hamdar helped with typing, editing, and scanning texts, as well as the preparation of the glossary and appendix. Michael Cooperson drew the pictures and made valuable suggestions after reading the first draft. Devin Stewart read the entire manuscript and gave valuable comments and suggestions. At Middlebury College, David Herren and his staff provided computer support and expertise, and Ernest Longie and his staff provided facilities and support for the recording of the audio tapes and duplication of the video tapes. John Samples, Director of Georgetown University Press, and Patricia Rayner, Production Manager, helped in preparing the final manuscript.

A special acknowledgment is due al-Ustaaz Abd el-Hakim El-Tonsi, director of the video scenes accompanying this book, and his staff for their dedicated and highly professional work in producing the video tape. The extra time and effort they put into filming and editing enabled us to complete the project on schedule.

Finally, we would like to express our thanks to the students of Arabic at Emory University, The College of William and Mary, and Middlebury College, who put up with the difficulties of working with very rough drafts of this book in 1992 and 1993, and to our colleagues who took on the challenge of working with new materials while under development. Their patience, encouragement, and enthusiasm have been inspirational.

ACKNOWLEDGMENTS

ALIF BAA

INTRODUCTION TO ARABIC LETTERS AND SOUNDS

ألف باء

مدخل الى حروف العربية وأصواتها

INTRODUCTION

The Arabic Alphabet

There are twenty-eight letters in the Arabic alphabet, and fourteen symbols that function as short vowels and pronunciation markers, or as markers of certain grammatical functions. Units One through Ten will introduce these letters and symbols individually. First, take a look at the alphabet as a whole. The following chart shows the twenty-eight letters. Starting in the upper right-hand corner, read across from right to left, which is the way Arabic is written and read. Listen to the tape as these sounds are pronounced.

(The tape symbol indicates that you should listen to the tape.)

ث	ت	ب	ا
د	خ	ح	ج
س	ز	ر	ذ
ط	ض	ص	ش
ف	غ	ع	ظ
م	ل	ك	ق
ي	و	هـ	ن

This chart shows the fourteen extra-alphabetical symbols and their names. They include short vowels, pronunciation symbols, grammatical endings, spelling variants, and a consonant that, for historical reasons, was not included with the letters of the alphabet. They will be introduced in Units One through Ten along with the letters of the alphabet.

ـُ Damma	ـَ fatHa
ـِ kasra	ـْ sukuun
ـّ shadda	ء hamza
آ madda	ة taa marbuuTa
ـٰ dagger alif	ٱ waSla
ـً tanwiin al-fatH	ـٌ tanwiin aD-Damm
ـٍ tanwiin al-kasr	ى alif maqSuura

Special Characteristics of the Arabic Script

The Arabic alphabet and writing system has four major characteristics that distinguish it from its European counterparts.

1. Arabic is written from right to left. One consequence of this ordering system is that books, newspapers, and magazines open and are read from right to left, rather than left to right.

2. Letters are connected in both print and handwriting, unlike those of the Latin alphabet, which are connected only in handwriting. The following are individual letters which are written one after the other in correct order, but which do not form a word written this way: ا ل ب ا ب . When they are connected, however, they do spell a word: الباب ("al-baab" *the door*). Notice that not all the letters in this word connect to the following letter. This is a characteristic of some of the letters; you will learn these rules as you learn to write each letter. In the following words, try to identify the nonconnecting letters:

لذيذ السودان زين اسد مبارك

As you learn the alphabet, note which letters connect and which do not, and when you practice writing, do not lift the pen or pencil from the page until you get to a natural break with a nonconnecting letter.

3. Letters have slightly different shapes depending on where they occur in a word. The chart on page 1 gives the forms of the letters when written independently; these forms vary when the letters are written in initial, medial, and final position. "Initial position" means not connected to a previous letter, "medial position" indicates that the letter is between two other letters, and "final position" means connected to the preceding letter. Most letters have a particularly distinct shape when they occur in final position, similar to the way English can have capital letters at the beginning of words. The chart on page 4 gives you an idea of the extent of this variation. You will see that each letter retains a basic shape throughout; this is the core of the letter. If the letter has dots, their number and position also remain the same. Note that the last three letters, which all connect, appear to have a "tail" in their independent and final forms which drops off when they are connected and is replaced by a connecting segment that rests on the line. Try to find the core shape of each letter, its dots, if any, the connecting segments, and the final tail in the following chart.

Final position	Medial Position	Initial Position	Independent
ـا	ـا	ا	ا
ـت	ـتـ	تـ	ت
ـج	ـجـ	جـ	ج
ـع	ـعـ	عـ	ع

As you learn each letter of the alphabet, you will learn to read and write all its various shapes. You will be surprised how quickly you master them, with a little practice!

4. Arabic script consists of two separate "layers" of writing. The basic skeleton of a word is made up of the consonants and long vowels. Short vowels and other pronunciation and grammatical markers are separated from the consonant skeleton of the word. This second layer, called vocalization, is normally omitted in writing, and the reader recognizes words without it. Compare the following two versions of the same text, a line of poetry, the first of which represents the normal way of writing, without vocalization, and the second of which has all the pronunciation markers added:

قفا نبك من ذكرى حبيب ومنزل   بسقط اللوى بين الدخول فحومل

قِفا نَبْكِ مِنْ ذِكْرَى حَبِيبٍ وَمَنْزِلِ   بِسِقْطِ ٱللِّوى بَيْنَ ٱلدَّخُولِ فَحَوْمَلِ

من معلقة امرئ القيس

Texts normally vocalized include elementary school textbooks, some editions of classical literary texts, and the Quran. In the Quran, the scripture of Islam, this precision has religious significance: the extra markings on the text leave no doubt as to the exact reading intended. Thus the text of the Quran shows full vocalization, as can be seen in the following excerpt.

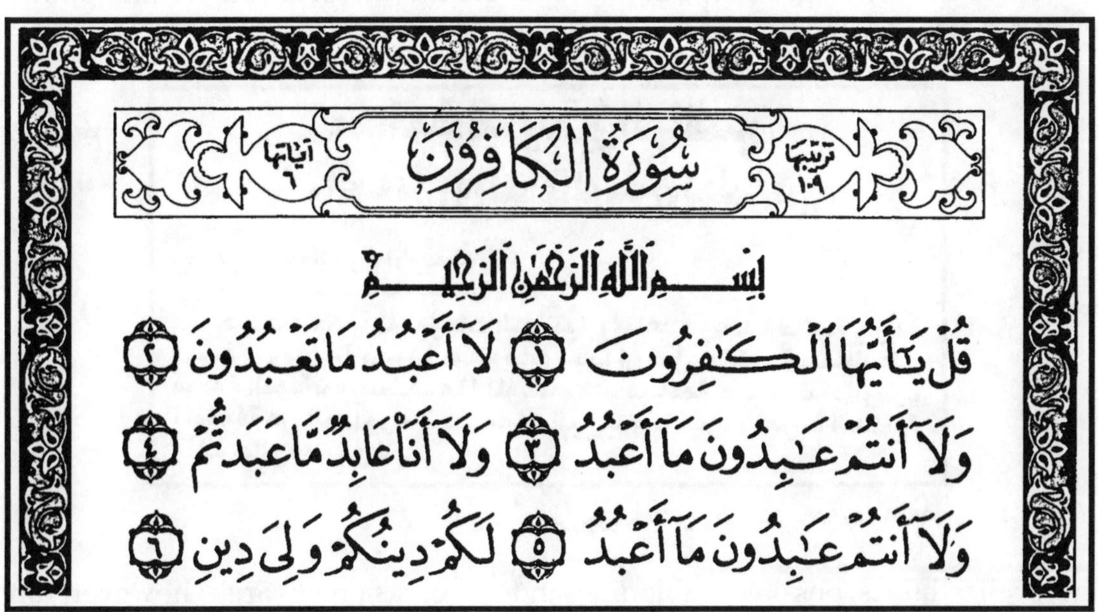

سُورَةُ الكَافِرُون

ترتيبها ١٠٩ — آياتها ٦

بِسْمِ ٱللَّهِ ٱلرَّحْمَٰنِ ٱلرَّحِيمِ

قُلْ يَٰٓأَيُّهَا ٱلْكَٰفِرُونَ ﴿١﴾ لَآ أَعْبُدُ مَا تَعْبُدُونَ ﴿٢﴾
وَلَآ أَنتُمْ عَٰبِدُونَ مَآ أَعْبُدُ ﴿٣﴾ وَلَآ أَنَا۠ عَابِدٌ مَّا عَبَدتُّمْ ﴿٤﴾
وَلَآ أَنتُمْ عَٰبِدُونَ مَآ أَعْبُدُ ﴿٥﴾ لَكُمْ دِينُكُمْ وَلِىَ دِينِ ﴿٦﴾

من القرآن الكريم، سورة "الكافرون"

In schoolbooks, vowel markings are used to introduce new vocabulary, and to enable the students to learn the correct pronunciation of formal Arabic, with all the correct grammatical endings. The following example is taken from a fourth-grade elementary reader.

كَرَمٌ عَرَبِيٌّ

فِي قَدِيمِ الزَّمانِ ، مَرَّتْ بِالْجَزِيرَةِ الْعَرَبِيَّةِ سَنَةُ مَحْلٍ قاسِيَةٌ ، فَلا مَطَرَ تَسْخُو بِهِ السَّماءُ، وَلا زَرْعَ تَجُودُ بِهِ الْأَرْضُ ، فَعَمَّ الْبُؤْسُ ، وَاشْتَدَّتِ الْحاجَةُ إِلَى الطَّعامِ . كانَ كُرَماءُ الْعَرَبِ يُساعِدُونَ الْمُحْتاجِينَ ، وَكانَ مِنْ أَكْرَمِهِمْ حاتِمٌ الطّائِيُّ .

من كتاب القراءة للصف الرابع الابتدائي ، ج. ٢، وزارة التربية السورية، ١٩٨٦

Thereafter, the students see the words in regular, unvocalized script. You will learn vocabulary the same way.

Most books, magazines, and newspapers are unvocalized, as the following newspaper article demonstrates.

محاكمة الجريدتين اللبنانيتين
«السفير» و«نداء الوطن» بعد غد

بيروت: «الشرق الأوسط»

حددت محكمة المطبوعات اللبنانية بعد غد موعداً لمحاكمة جريدة «السفير» بتهمة نشرها «معلومات يجب ان تبقى مكتومة حفاظا على سلامة الدولة». ويصادف هذا الموعد، موعد محاكمة جريدة «نداء الوطن» الموقوفة عن الصدور منذ بضعة اسابيع بتهمة اثارة النعرات الطائفية والمس بالوحدة الوطنية.

من جريدة الشرق الاوسط ، ١٨/٥/١٩٩٣

In unvocalized texts, possible ambiguities in form occasionally arise; however, rarely does this result in ambiguous meaning.

In this textbook series, vocalization marks will be used when new vocabulary is introduced, but thereafter you will be expected to have memorized the pronunciation of the word, and these marks will be omitted. Since Arabic speakers normally read and write without vocalization, it is best to become accustomed to reading and writing that way from the beginning.

Pronunciation of Arabic

In addition to the characteristics of the Arabic script, you should also be aware of certain features of the sounds of Arabic.

1. Arabic has a one-to-one correspondence between sound and letter, whereas English spelling often uses one letter or combination of letters to represent several different sounds. Consider the plural marker *s* in the words *dogs* and *books*, and note that the sound of the first is actually *z*, not *s*. Compare also the two different sounds spelled as *th* as in *think* and *those*. These are two distinct sounds, and Arabic has two different letters to represent them. American English speakers sometimes confuse pronunciation and spelling without realizing it. For example, think about the word *television*. This word has been adopted into Arabic and is pronounced something like *televizyoon*. It is also spelled with the Arabic letter that corresponds to the sound *z*, because that it the way it is pronounced. English spelling, on the other hand, requires an *s*, even though there is no *s* sound in the word. Pay attention to the sounds of the Arabic letters, and avoid associating English letters with them so that you will not confuse the two.

2. The Arabic writing system is regularly phonetic, which means that words are generally written as they are pronounced. Learn to recognize and pronounce the sounds correctly now, and not only will you avoid spelling problems, but you will also learn and retain vocabulary more easily.

3. In general, Arabic sounds use a wider range of mouth and throat positions than English. Be aware of what parts of the mouth you must use to produce these sounds properly from the beginning, when you are able to focus the most attention on them. You will learn to make new sounds, and to do so, you must become familiar with a set of muscles that you use to make sounds like gargling or coughing but not to speak English. Your muscles are capable of making all these sounds, but you must become conscious of what they are doing and you must practice. Just as you must train your arm to hit a tennis ball, you must train your throat to contract or tighten, and this takes constant repetition. You must keep your eye on the ball in tennis, and you must keep your mind on the sounds you are making at all times. With practice, you will gradually be able to do this with less and less effort.

Units One through Ten

In Units One through Ten, you will learn the basics of reading, writing, and speaking Arabic. Listen to the tape as you read, make a habit of pronouncing *out loud* everything you write while you are writing it, and practice on your own in addition to doing the drills in the book. The more time you put in now, the less you will have to spend later!

الوحدة الاولى
UNIT ONE

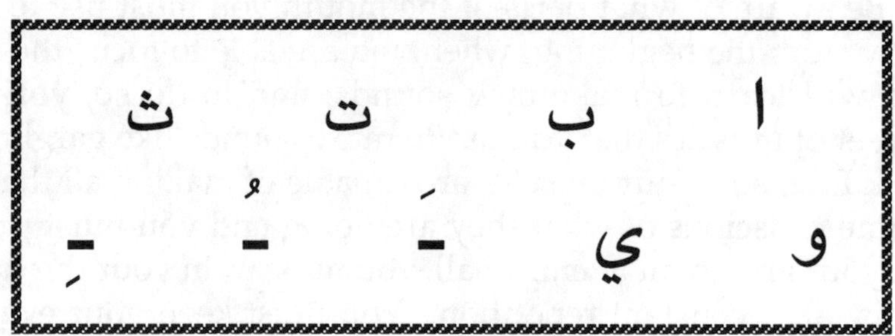

This unit will introduce you to the first four letters of the Arabic alphabet and to the long and short vowels.

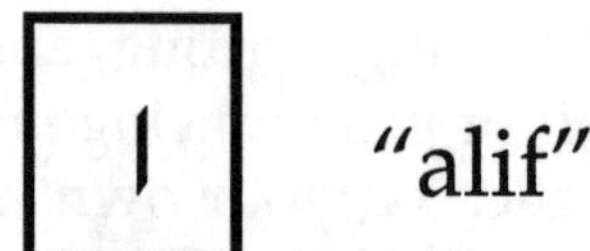

The name of the first letter of the Arabic alphabet is *alif.* Alif has two main functions, the first of which will be introduced in this unit, and the second in Unit Three. Here we are concerned with its function as a long vowel, whose pronunciation resembles that of *a* in *bad* or in *father*. Say these two words aloud and notice the difference in the quality of the *a*: the former is pronounced in the front of the mouth, and the latter is deeper and farther back. The pronunciation of alif has this same range. Two factors influence the quality of alif: regional dialect and surrounding consonants. In the Gulf region (Saudi Arabia, Kuwait, Iraq, and neighboring countries), the sound is generally deeper, closer to *father*, while farther west, in the Mediterranean area, it is more frontal, closer to *bad*. In addition, certain "emphatic" consonant sounds that are pronounced farther back in the mouth can also deepen the sound of alif so that it resembles *father.* Learning to discern and produce the difference in vowel quality will help you understand, speak, and write Arabic accurately.

Listening Exercise 1.

To hear the two variants of alif, listen to the following pairs of words on tape. You should be able to distinguish between the frontal alif and the deep alif (remember that the words are read from right to left):

تاب / طاب　　ساح / صاح　　داني / ضاني　　ذال / ظالم

Notice that the first word in each pair above begins with a sound comparable to an English one, whereas the second word begins with a sound that resembles the former but is pronounced with the tongue lower and farther back in the mouth. These latter sounds are called "emphatic" consonants, and they affect the pronunciation of the alif. Listening for the difference between frontal and deep alif is the best way to distinguish between emphatic and nonemphatic consonants. We will discuss this point in more depth later when you begin learning the emphatic letters. In the meantime, pay attention to the quality of alif in the words you hear.

Drill 1.

You will hear twelve words. For each, note whether the alif is frontal (F) or deep (D):

1. D	5. F	9. F
2. F	6. F	10. D
3. D	7. D	11. F
4. D	8. F	12. D

In addition to listening for vowel quality, you must also learn to recognize **vowel length.** Alif is a long vowel, which means that it must be distinguished from its short counterpart, the fatHa (short *a* vowel). The length of a long vowel should be **at least twice** that of a short vowel. Remember that English has no long vowels, so Arabic long vowels should sound and feel extra long to you. Do not worry about pronouncing a long vowel "too long"—stretch it out so that you can feel the difference.

Listening Exercise 2.

Listen to the differences in vowel **quality and length** in the following pairs of words. The first word in each pair contains an alif, and the second a fatHa. Notice that the alif ranges in sound from *a* in *bad* (frontal) to *a* in *father* (deep), while the fatHa ranges from *e* in *bet* (frontal) to *u* in *but* (deep):

بات / بَت   ساد / سَد   شاب / شَب   بار / بَر   قال / قَل

Drill 2.

You will hear twelve words. Mark **A** if you hear alif, or **F** if you hear fatHa.

1. A	5. F	9. A
2. F	6. A	10. A
3. A	7. F	11. F
4. A	8. F	12. A

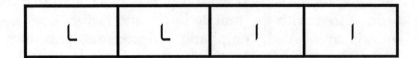

Writing

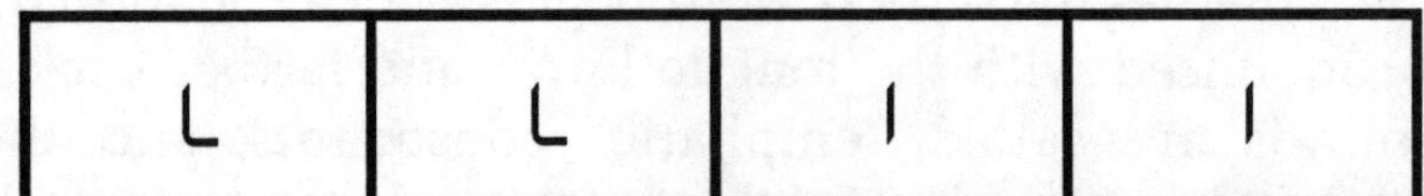

In this section you will learn to write the various shapes of the letter alif. The box above contains, reading right to left, the independent, initial, medial, and final shapes of this letter. Alone or at the beginning of a word, the alif is written as a single stroke, drawn from top to bottom, as the arrow in the example shows. Practice on the blank lines below, as shown in the example on the first line, pronouncing alif as you write it. Write the letter as many times as you can in the space provided:

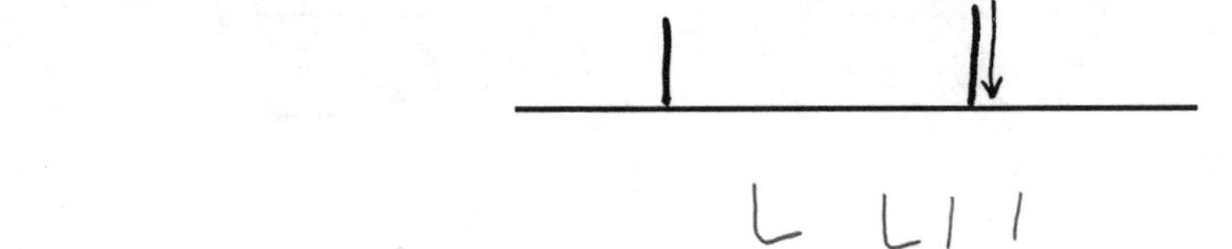

When the alif follows another letter, it is written from the bottom up. The previous letter will end in a connecting segment drawn on the line. Start with that segment, then draw the alif from the bottom up as shown:

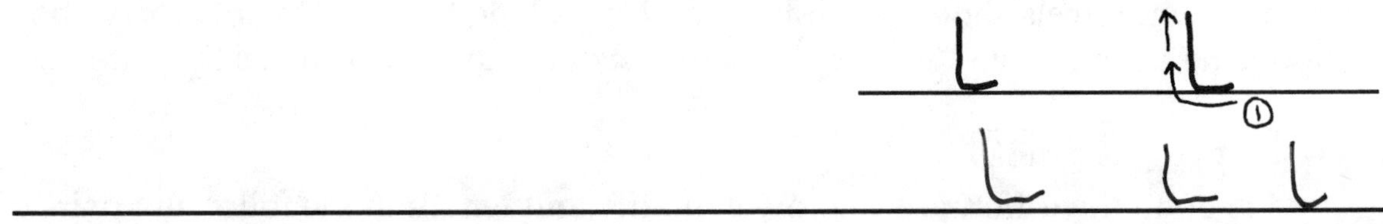

In either case, **the alif does not connect to what follows it.** After writing the alif, pick your pen up from the page, and start the next letter as if it were the beginning of a new word.

Now practice reading alif by circling all of the alifs you can find in the following sentence (taken from *1001 Nights*):

كان يا ما كان في قديم الزمان، كان تاجر كثير المال والاعمال ...

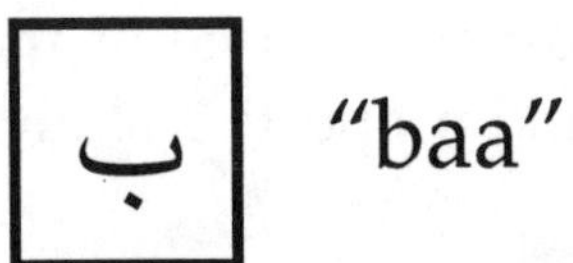

"baa"

The second letter of the Arabic alphabet is pronounced like English *b*.

Listening Exercise 3.

Listen to and repeat the following words that contain the sound ب :

باء　　باب　　لبنان　　ليبيا　　بيت　　حب

Writing

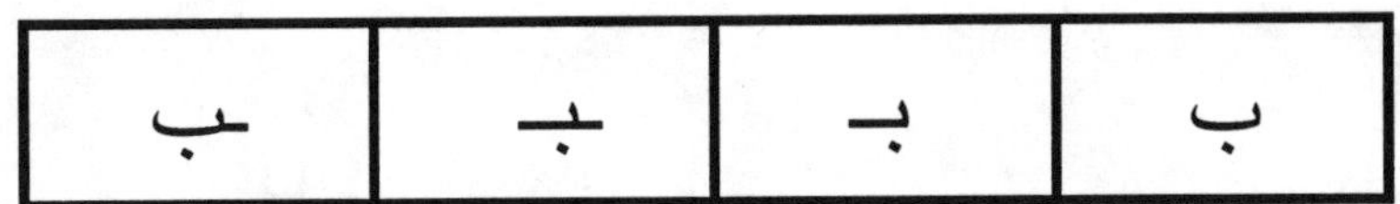

Unlike ا , ب is a **connecting** letter, which means that **it connects to the letter following it** when it occurs at the beginning or in the middle of a word. The four shapes in the box above represent ب in independent, initial, medial, and final positions. Notice that the main parts of the letter, the initial tooth and the dot beneath the body, remain constant in all four shapes. Compare the independent and final shapes, and note that both end in a second tooth. Remember that many letters take a characteristic "tail" shape in independent and final positions. You can see that this second tooth is the tail of the ب . It is not written in initial and medial positions because ب connects to the following letter in those cases.

When written alone, this letter takes the shape shown at the far right above. Following the steps shown in the example on the first line below, trace the letter with your pencil a few times, then write it. First, write the body: from right to left, begin with a small hook, then continue straight along the line and end with another hook for the tail. After you have finished the body, place the dot underneath as shown.

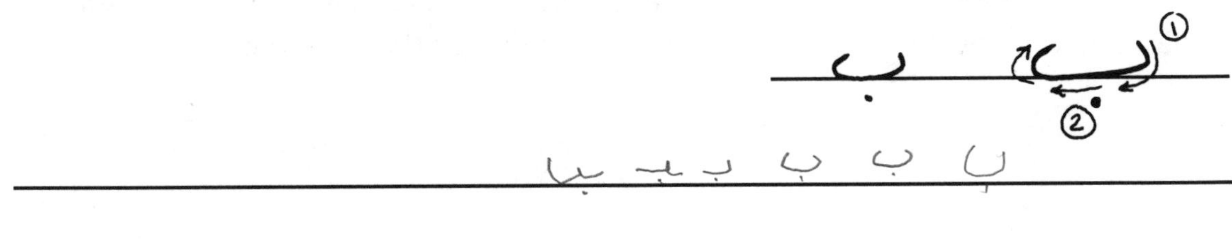

When ب is followed by another letter, it connects to that letter by dropping the final hook: بـ . The exact length of the body depends on the style of the handwriting or print font and may vary a little; copy the size and proportion shown in the example:

You can now write the first two letters of the alphabet joined together: با . When writing words in Arabic, dots are written last, like dotting the *i* and crossing the *t* when writing in cursive English. Copy the example, pronouncing it each time you write:

When ب occurs in medial position, that is, when connected بـ follows a connecting letter, the connecting segment of that letter connects into the hook at the beginning like this: ـبـ . Copy the example:

Final ب resembles the independent form with the final hook. This form may be illustrated by writing two ب 's together: بب . Copy the example:

Now you can write your first word in Arabic: باب *door*. Practice writing this word by copying the example shown below, pronouncing it out loud as you write. **Remember:** do not stop to dot the letters until you have finished the skeletal structure of the entire word.

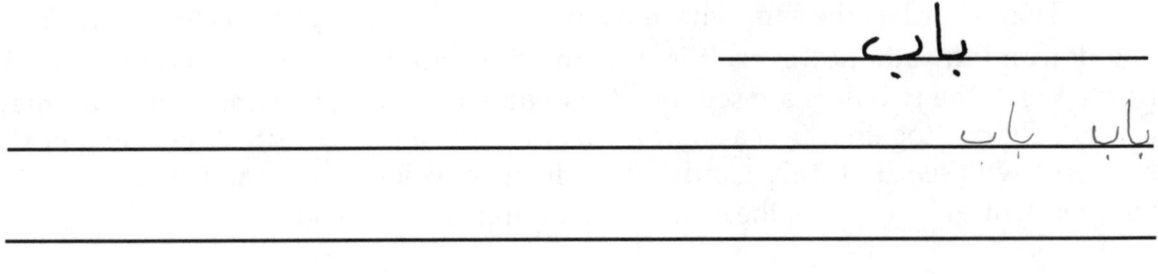

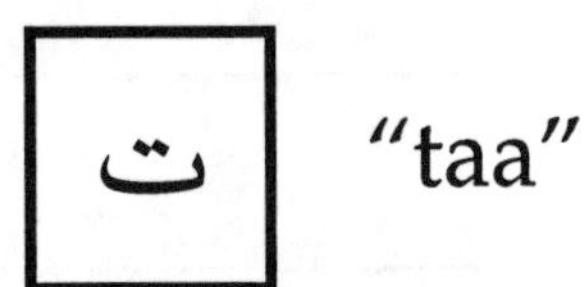

"taa"

The third letter of the alphabet is pronounced like a clear, frontal English *t*. How many different ways do you pronounce *t*? Read the following list aloud the way you would normally pronounce the words when speaking: *bottle, teeth, automatic.* Of these words, most American speakers pronounce the *t* in *teeth* farther forward in the mouth, against the back of the teeth. This is the correct position of the tongue for the pronunciation of this Arabic sound; do not confuse it with the flap of the tongue you use to produce *automatic.* Arabic ت must be pronounced with the tip of your tongue against your teeth, but without aspiration.[1] Since ت is a frontal letter, the vowel sounds surrounding it are frontal too; in particular, the alif and fatHa (short *a*) are pronounced like *a* in *bad* and *e* as in *bet* (**not** like *a* in *father* and *u* in *but*).

Listening Exercise 4.

Listen to the letter ت in the following words and repeat. Pay attention to the position of your tongue as you do so and notice the frontal quality of the vowels:

تاء　　بات　　توت　　وتد　　بنت　　شتاء

---

[1]Aspiration refers to the breathy sound often heard with *t, p,* and *k.* Light a match, hold it in front of your mouth, and say, *Peter, Tom, and Kirk went to town.* The flame will flicker each time you pronounce one of these letters. Arabic sounds do not have aspiration, so practice saying *t* and *k* with a lit match in front of your mouth until you can pronounce them without making the flame flicker.

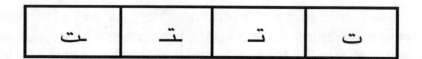

Writing

This letter has the same shape as the ب , and is also a connector. Instead of one dot underneath, however, it is written with two dots above its body: ت . In printed text, the two dots are separated, as you see. In handwriting, however, they are usually run together into a short horizontal bar. (Try to write two dots quickly and you will see how this handwriting form developed!) Practice writing the independent ت by copying the example, pronouncing it as you write:

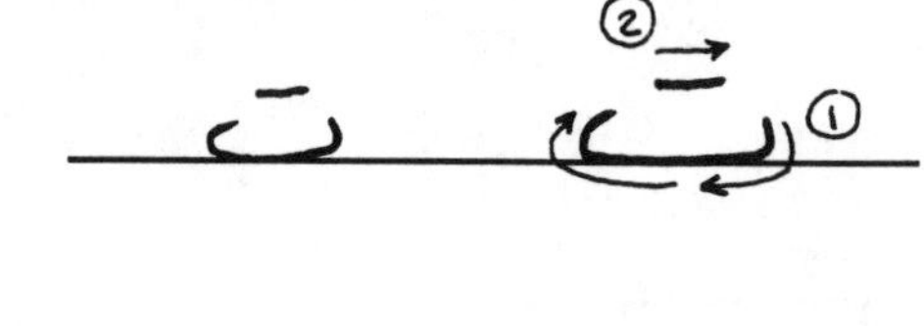

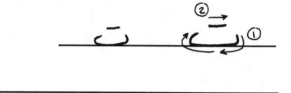

Now practice writing ت in initial and medial positions by copying the word تتب (*tatub*) as shown:

Practice writing ت in final position by copying the word بت (*bit*):

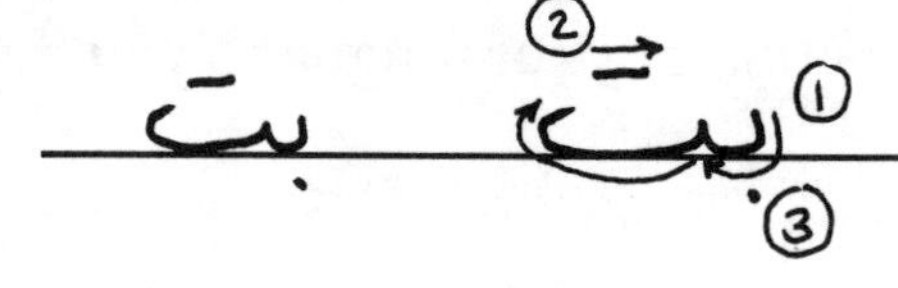

Drill 3.

Dictation. Write the six words you hear on tape. Listen to each word as many times as necessary.

1. ______________　　　　4. ______________

2. ______________　　　　5. ______________

3. ______________　　　　6. ______________

ث "thaa"

The next letter is pronounced like the first sound in *three*. **Do not** associate this sound with the English letters *th,* because the English spelling represents two quite distinct sounds, each of which has an Arabic equivalent. Pronounce *three* and *that* out loud several times and compare the way you pronounce them. The letter ث represents the sound in *three,* **not** the sound in *that.* Remember this by reminding yourself that this letter has *three* dots. If necessary, say *three* out loud before pronouncing or reading ث .

Drill 4.

Make sure you know the difference between the sounds in *three* and *that.* Say the following words out loud and group them below according to the sound they contain:

they	*thumb*	*teeth*	*there*	*throb*	*thus*
although	*think*	*through*	*brother*	*together*	*thought*
weather	*bother*	*theft*	*then*	*depth*	*rather*

three : ____

that : ____

Listening Exercise 5.

Listen to the letter ث in these words and repeat:

ثاء　　　ثابت　　　تثبت　　　اثاث　　　بث　　　مثال

Writing

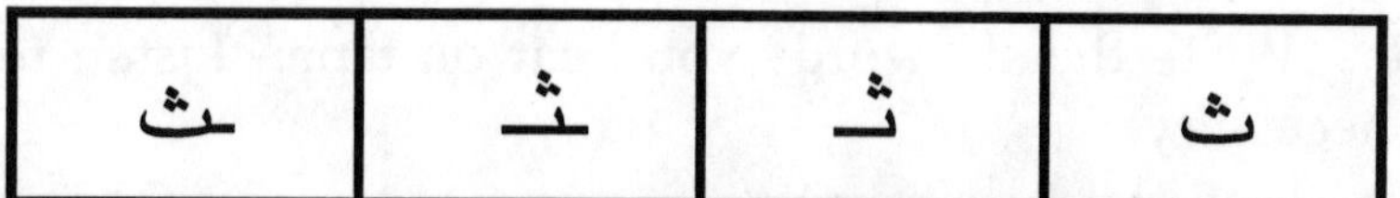

This letter is a connector, and is written just like ب and ت in all positions, except that it takes three dots above. In print, the three dots appear as you see above; in handwriting, the three dots are usually connected and written as a caret-shaped mark as shown in the example. Practice writing and saying independent ث:

Copy and practice initial ثـ in the male name ثابت (*Thaabit*):

Practice writing medial ـثـ in the word تثبت (*tathbut*):

Write final ـث by copying the word تبث (*tabuth*):

Drill 5. ⊗⊗

You will hear six words. Circle the word that you hear in each line:

1.	باب	بات	4.	تب	بث
2.	ثبات	بتات	5.	باثث	ثابت
3.	ثاب	تاب	6.	ثبت	تبت

!برافـو (*Bravo!*) You have learned the first four letters of the Arabic alphabet. The next letters in sequence will be presented in Unit Two. Now we will skip ahead to the other two long vowels, and the symbols for the corresponding short vowels.

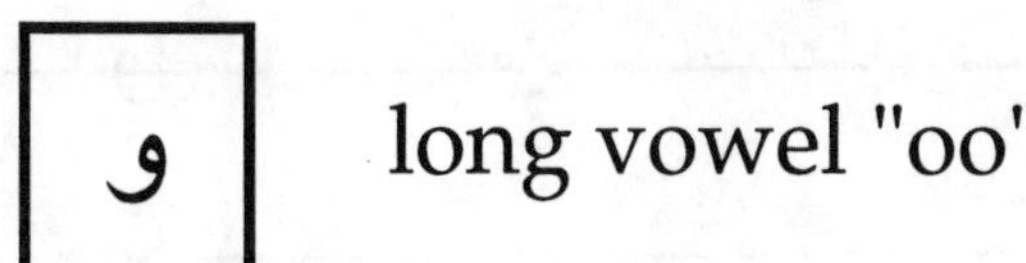

This letter represents the second of the three long vowels in Arabic. It is pronounced like the exclamation of delight: *ooooo!* Practice saying this sound and stretch it out, just like you would the exclamation. Remember that the pronunciation of و, like that of alif, should be **twice as long** as normal English vowels.

Listening Exercise 6. ⊗⊗

Listen to and repeat the following words containing و:

سـورة   تحبو   تـونـس   ثبـوت   تابـوت   تـوت

Writing

ـو	ـو	و	و

As you can see in the chart above, the shapes of و do not vary much. Like ا, و does not connect to a following letter. To write independent or initial و, start on the line, loop clockwise to the left and up, then swing down into the tail, which should dip well below the line. Copy the example:

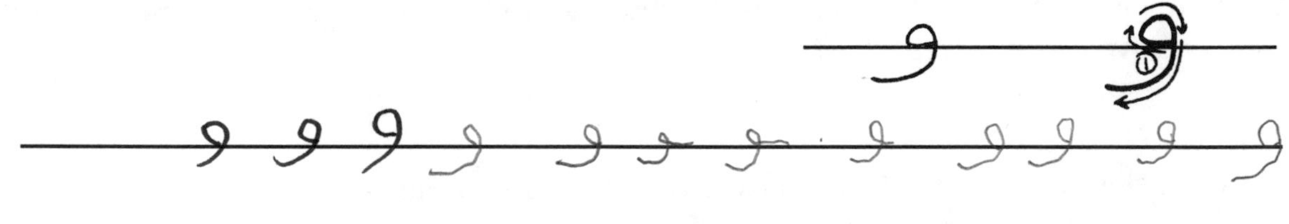

When writing و connected to a previous letter, the joining segment leads into the beginning point of the loop. Copy the example:

ـو و

Now practice writing and pronouncing some of the words you heard above. Copy the examples:

توت   توت   تابوت   تابوت   ثبوت   ثبوت

Drill 6.

Dictation. Write the words you hear on tape.

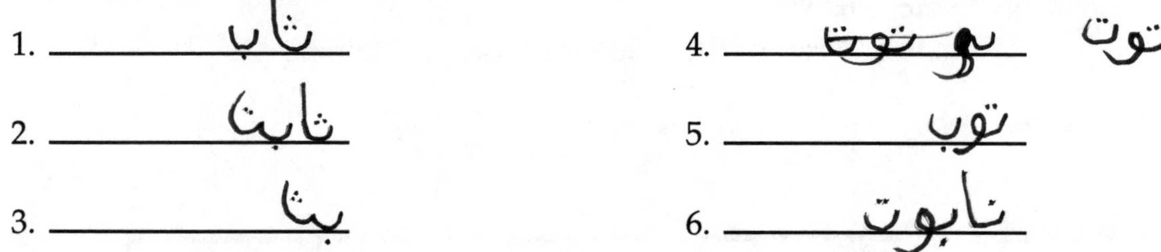

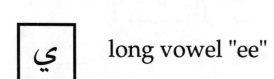

ي long vowel "ee"

This letter represents the last of the three long vowels, the sound of *ee* in *beep*. Remember that this is a long vowel—hold this sound for **twice as long** as you would hold *ee* in words like *beep*, *street*, etc.

Listening Exercise 7.

Listen to and repeat the following words containing ي:

توبي   تثبيت   ليبي   تثبتي   دين   ديك

Writing

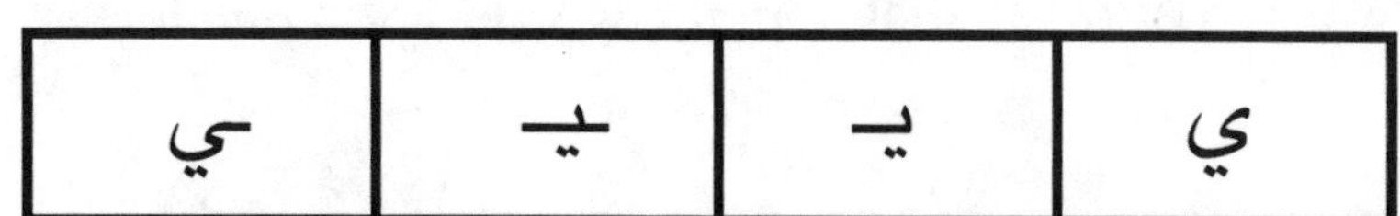

As you can see in the box, the independent and final forms of ي differ slightly from the initial and medial forms. Like ب , ت , and ث , which it resembles in its initial and medial shapes, this letter is a connecting one. All shapes of ي retain the two dots below, but, in handwriting, the two dots underneath are usually drawn as a short horizontal bar, just like the dots on top of ت .

To write independent ي , start above the line, and make the top half of an *s* down to the line. Continue below the line into a wide, flat curve as shown, **making sure to bring the tail all the way back up over the line:**

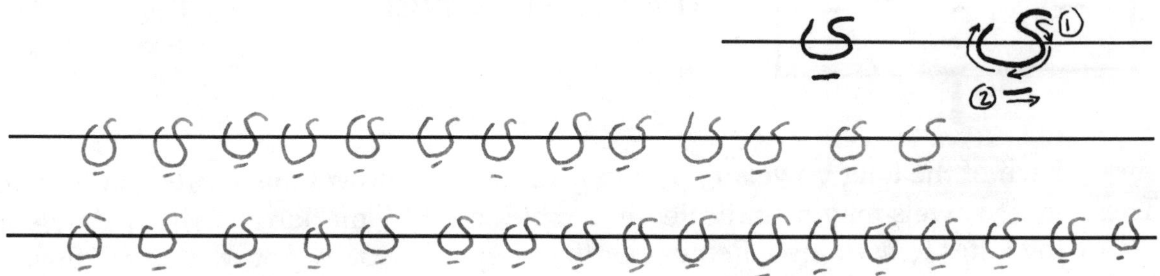

In final position, start from the connecting segment on the line, then make a small hook into the body. In this position, the letter is almost entirely below the line, and has only a small curved hook before dipping into the wide flat curve. Practice copying and pronouncing ـي **and bring the tail all the way back up over the line:**

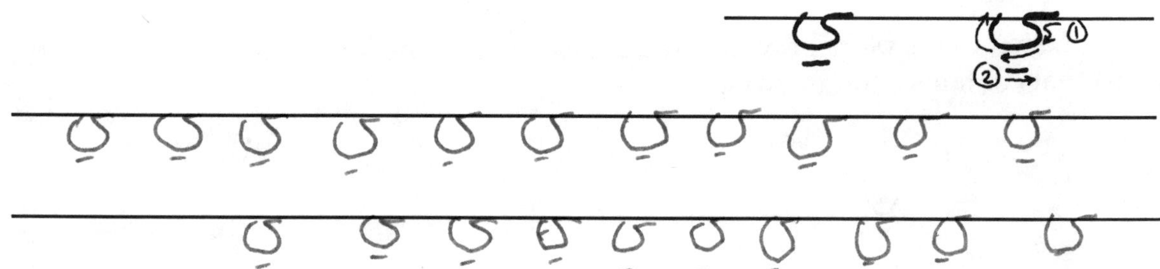

When ي occurs at the beginning or in the middle of a word, it takes the same shape as ت , except that its two dots are below the body of the letter. Copy the example of initial يـ :

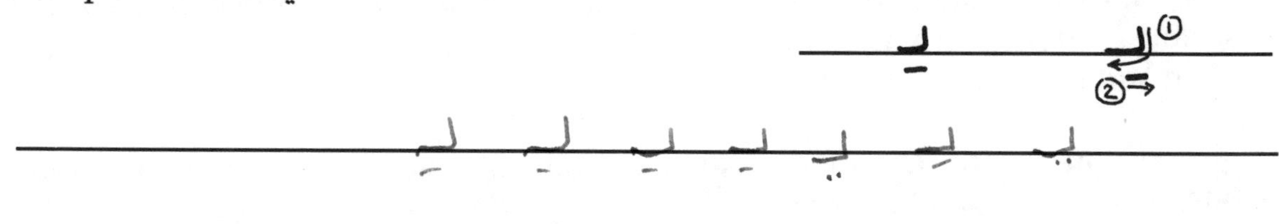

Now practice writing medial ـبـ in the word تثبيت (*tathbeet*):

ـَ ـُ ـِ

the short vowels

Each of the long vowels ا , و , and ي has a short vowel that corresponds to it. These short vowels may be indicated in Arabic script by markings written above or below the letter they follow. Remember that they are usually not written at all; you have been writing words without them so far. The length of the short vowels corresponds to the length of most English vowels, and the length of the long vowels should be at least double that. It is important to learn to distinguish between the two lengths in listening and in speaking, for that difference often marks a difference in meaning.

Drill 7.

Listen to the pairs of words and repeat. Circle the letter corresponding to the word that contains a long vowel.

1.	a	b	4.	a	b
2.	a	b	5.	a	b
3.	a	b	6.	a	b

Syllables in Arabic always begin with a consonant. By convention, short vowels are written above or below the consonant they follow. Writing vowels is the third and final step in writing a word—if they are written at all—after both the skeleton and the dots have been completed.

The names of the short vowels are fatHa, Damma, and kasra. They correspond to long vowels *aa*, *oo*, and *ee* respectively.

"fatHa"

The short vowel that corresponds to alif is called fatHa. Like its long counterpart alif, fatHa ranges in quality from frontal to deep, depending on the quality of the consonants surrounding it. In its most frontal position, fatHa sounds like English *e* as in *bed*. Deep fatHa sounds like English *u* in *but*. Consonants ت , ب , and ث are frontal ones, so they give fatHa a frontal quality, like *e* in *bed*.

Listening Exercise 8.

Listen to and repeat the following words that contain alif and fatHa. Pay special attention to the difference in vowel length.

ثابَت　　　تابَ　　　باتَت　　　تابَت　　　ثَبات

FatHa is written as a small slanted dash above the consonant it follows, as in the example ثَبَتَ . Copy:

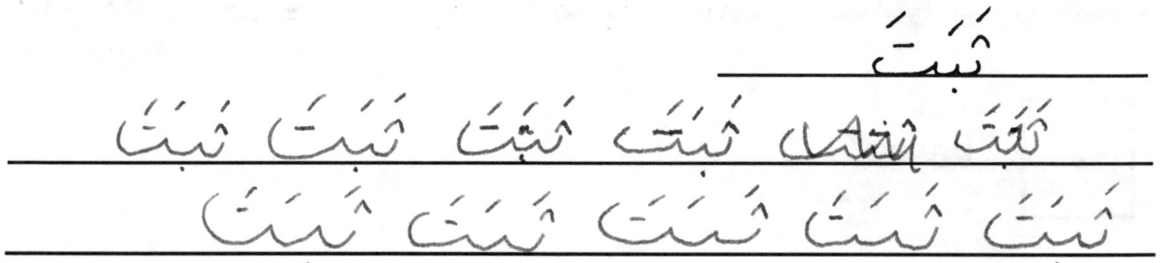

Drill 8.

Listen to the words on tape, and write ـَ where you hear it:

1. تثبيت　　　3. بات　　　5. ثبت

2. بتات　　　4. ثبات　　　6. ثابت

"Damma"

The short vowel that corresponds to و is called Damma, and is pronounced like *oo* as in *booth* when following frontal consonants. When it is affected by deep consonants, it is a little bit deeper, somewhat like *oo* in *wool*.

Listening Exercise 9.

Listen to and repeat the following words containing Damma:

تُب   بُث   ثُبوت   حُبوب   صُب   تَثبُت

Make a special effort to pronounce this vowel clearly, and **do not confuse it with English** *o* and *u*, which represent many different sounds, few of which resemble ـُ. For example, *u* in words like *but* and *gum* actually represents the sound of a deep fatHa, **not** a Damma.

Damma is written like a miniature و on top of the letter it follows, as in the word تُب. Practice writing ـُ as shown:

ـِ "kasra"

The short vowel that corresponds to ي is called kasra, and its pronunciation ranges from frontal *ee* as in *keep* to deep *i* as in *bit*. As with fatHa and Damma, the exact pronunciation of kasra depends on surrounding consonants. Frontal consonants like ت and ث give kasra a frontal quality.

Listening Exercise 10.

Listen to and repeat the following words containing kasra:

ثِب   تثبِتي   بِت   طِب   تحِب   كِتابي

Kasra is written as a small slanted dash under the letter it follows, as in ثِب. Copy the example:

Drill 9.

In the following schoolbook text, find five examples of each the short vowels and circle all the consonants you recognize.

> ## كُرَةُ السَّلَّة
>
> نَزَلَ التَّلاميذُ إلى مَلعَبِ المَدرَسَةِ فَرِحينَ ، والحَماسَةُ تَملأُ نُفوسَهُم. فَدَرسُ الرِّياضَةِ اليَومَ مُباراةٌ في كُرَةِ السَّلَّةِ ، بَينَ فَريقِ القُمصانِ الحَمراءِ ، وفَريقِ القُمصانِ الخَضراءِ .

من كتاب القراءة للصف الرابع الابتدائي ، ج. ٢، وزارة التربية السورية، ١٩٨٦

Drill 10.

You will hear twelve words. For each, mark **L** if you hear one of the long vowels (ا , و , or ي). Mark **S** if the word has only short vowels (fatHa, Damma, or kasra).

1. L	5. L	9. L
2. S	6. S	10. L
3. L	7. S	11. L
4. S	8. S	12. S

Drill 11.

Listen to the following words on tape and write the short vowels that you hear:

1. ثبتت	3. تبيت	5. تثبت
2. تبت	4. تتوب	6. ثبوت

Drill 12.

Dictation. Write the words you hear on tape.

1. ________ 5. ________

2. ________ 6. ________

3. ________ 7. ________

4. ________ 8. ________

Drill 13.

Read the following words aloud:

1. بَث	5. ثَبات	9. توبي
2. بابي	6. تَبات	10. تيتو
3. تُثبِت	7. تابا	11. ثابَت
4. ثُب	8. ثابِت	12. تَثبيت

Read and learn this word:

باب

Drill 14.

Connect the letters to form words, as shown in the example. Sound the words out as you write them.

Example: تاب ______ = ت + ا + ب

1. ______ = ب + ا + ت + ا

2. ______ = ثَ + ب + ا + ت + ي

3. ______ = ب + ا + ب + ا

4. ______ = ثَ + بَ + تَ

5. ______ = ب + ا + ب + ي

6. ______ = ت + و + ب + ي

7. ______ = تُ + ب + تَ

8. ______ = ت + و + ب + ا

9. ______ = تُ + ث + بِ + ت + ي

10. ______ = تَ + ب + ي + ت

11. ______ = ب + ي + ت + ي

CULTURE الثقافة 

In this section you will learn greetings and frequently used phrases in the spoken Arabic of Cairo by watching a video tape with your teacher. The scenes you will watch were filmed in Cairo and are meant to provide an introduction to certain aspects of Arab culture. We have chosen the Cairene dialect because it is the most widely understood dialect in the Arab world, and because almost one in every three Arabs is Egyptian. A few of the words you will learn from the dialogues may vary slightly in other dialects, but the transition is not difficult to make. (If you have friends from other countries, you can ask them to teach you the varieties they use.)

Watch the scenes with your teacher, who will help you understand and learn the expressions. Watch each dialogue several times, first to understand what is being said, and then to concentrate on exactly **how** it is being said. Remember that you learned your native language by listening and imitating!

VIDEO

Watch Scenes 1 and 2 on the video tape with your teacher.

HADRITAK / HADRITIK

In Egypt, when meeting someone for the first time, or addressing someone senior to you in age or position, or someone you do not know well, it is impolite to address him or her as "you." Address men with the word *HaDritak* (literally *your presence*), and women with *HaDritik*, to show respect.

الوحدة الثانية

UNIT TWO

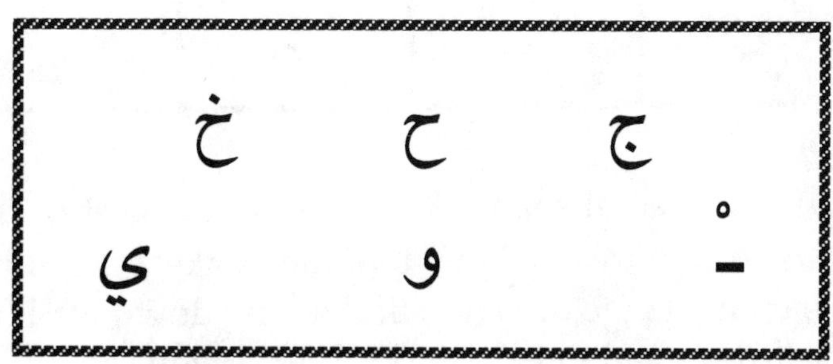

In this unit you will learn three more consonants, more about the letters و and ي , and the symbol that indicates the absence of a short vowel. Two of the three consonant sounds have no English equivalent. Learn to pronounce them properly now, and practice to develop the muscles you use to pronounce these sounds. Try to spend five or ten minutes, three times a day, practicing these sounds with the tape.

The three consonants in the first line of the box above represent the next three letters in the alphabet after ث . Just as ب , ت , and ث share the same skeletal shape and are distinguished by the number and position of the dots, so these three letters have the same basic shapes, but are distinguished by their dots.

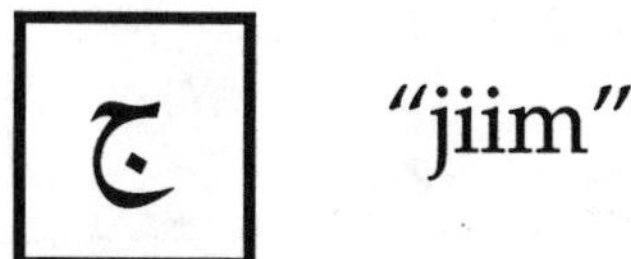

This letter has three different pronunciations that vary according to region in the Arab world. In the Arabian Peninsula and the Gulf, it is pronounced like *j* in *jack* or *dg* in *bridge*. In most of the Levant and North Africa, it is pronounced like the French *j* in *bonjour* (a sound often represented in English by *s* as in *pleasure* or *decision*). In Cairo, it is pronounced like the hard *g* in *game*.

Listening Exercise 1.

Listen to the following words on tape as they are pronounced each way in turn:

جابِر　　تاج　　جُب　　دَجاج　　تُجيب

It is important to learn to recognize all three pronunciations of ج , but choose one to use when speaking.

WRITING

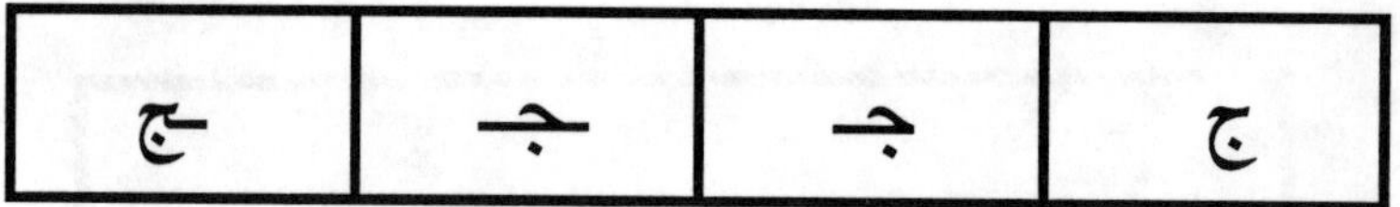

As the initial and medial shapes of this letter suggest, ج is a connector. To write ج alone, start at a point well above the line, make a small hook, then draw a line straight across, then change direction and swing down well below the line into the tail. Follow the arrows and imitate the shape that you see:

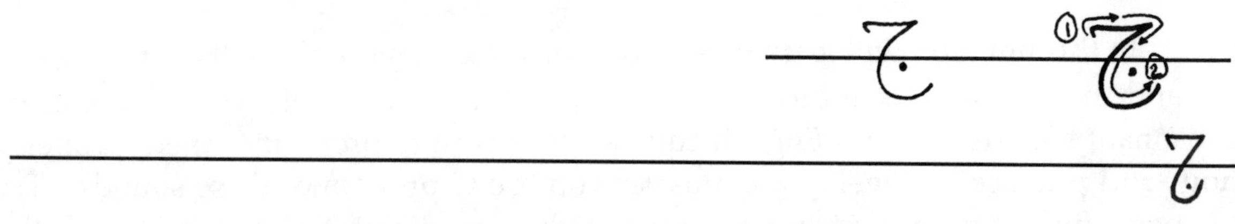

To write ج in initial position, begin with the hook as you did above, then slant down toward the line into a point just above the line, and then, instead of curving down into the tail, continue into the connecting segment as shown:

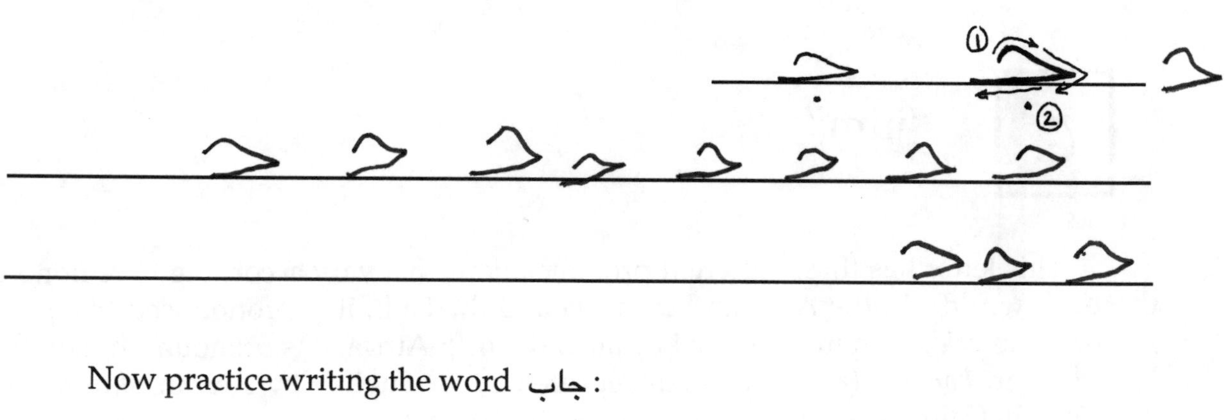

Now practice writing the word جاب :

جاب

جاب جاب

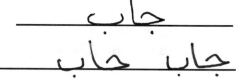

When this letter is connected on both sides, it takes the following shape in printed text: ـجـ as in تـجـيـب . **However, it is not written this way by hand.** To write this letter in the middle of a word, you must plan ahead, because the connecting segment lies well above the line, at the highest point of this letter. This means that you need to end the previous letter above the line. In the following example, the combination تجـ is written by starting and drawing the تـ completely above the line into the ـجـ . Copy the word تجيب as it is written here:

In word-final position, ج takes the same tail it has independently. Notice that, to reach the starting point of final ـج , a connecting segment is drawn from the line up and then over as the example shows. Copy the word بيج as it is written here:

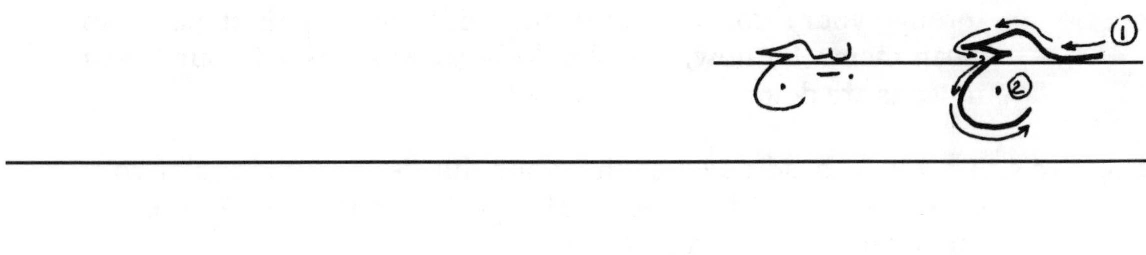

Drill 1.
Dictation.

1. ____________ 4. ____________

2. ____________ 5. ____________

3. ____________ 6. ____________

ح "Haa"

This letter represents a sound that is pronounced deep in the throat. It has no equivalent in English. First, take a few minutes to become better acquainted with some of your throat muscles that you use often, but not to speak English. The following exercises are designed to make you aware of what these muscles can already do, so that you can use them to speak Arabic. Practice them for a few minutes every day, as often as you can.

Exercise 1. With your mouth closed, block off your windpipe at your throat. Put your hand on your throat at the Adam's apple and constrict the muscles on the inside. You should be able to feel the muscles contracting. Alternately tighten and relax them for a few minutes.

Exercise 2. Repeat this with your mouth open. Try to breathe out through your mouth—if you can, you are not closing off the windpipe entirely.

Exercise 3. Constrict those same muscles so that air can just barely squeeze through your throat. Imitate someone fogging a pair of glasses to clean them. By now, you should be aware of what your throat muscles are doing.

Exercise 4. Bend your head down so that your chin rests on the top of your chest, and repeat Exercise 3. This position should make it easier for you to feel what you are doing.

Pronouncing ح takes practice, first to pronounce the letter alone, and then to pronounce it surrounded by other letters in a word. You must learn to pronounce it properly to be understood, and at first, this will take some concentration on your part. However, the more you practice now, the sooner you will be able to say it easily.

Listening Exercise 2.

Listen to the sound of ح in various positions and imitate:

حَبيب　　بَحث　　تَبوح　　حال　　حُدود　　صَباح

Writing

ح	ـحـ	حـ	ـح

Like ج , ح is a connector. It is written exactly like ج , except that it has no dot. Practice writing initial ح in the male name حَبيب :

Now practice writing and pronouncing medial ـحـ in تَحت (*below*). Remember to plan ahead and write the preceding letter above the line so that you can begin ـحـ from above. Copy:

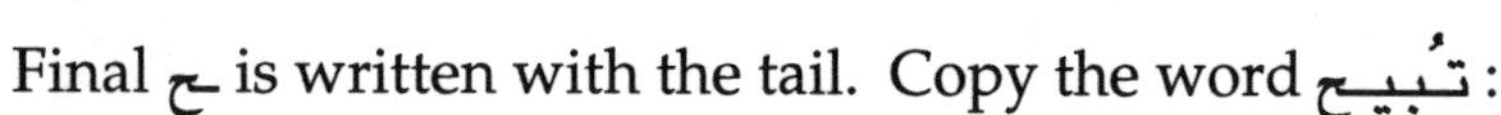

Final ـح is written with the tail. Copy the word تُبيح :

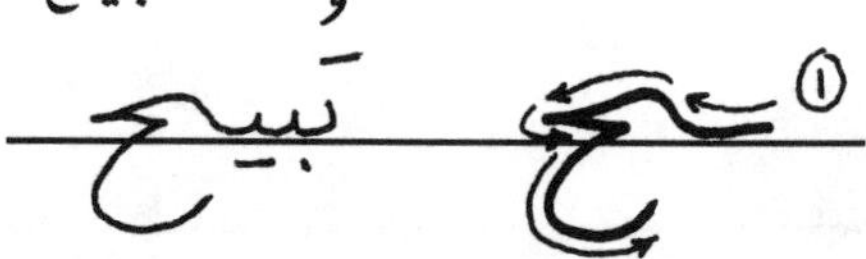

Drill 2.

Dictation.

1. ____________________ 4. ____________________

2. ____________________ 5. ____________________

3. ____________________ 6. ____________________

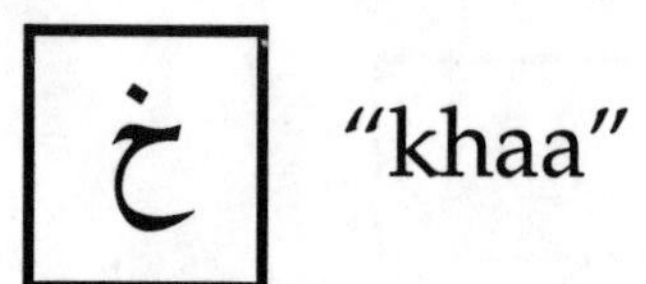

خ "khaa"

The sound of this letter is found in many European languages: the Russian *x*, the Scottish pronunciation of *loch*, and German *ch* as pronounced after a back vowel as in *Bach*. Some people use this sound to say *yech!* To pronounce خ, say *k* and pay attention to where the back of your tongue hits the back of the roof of your mouth and blocks your windpipe. Instead of closing off the windpipe with the back of your tongue completely, block it part way, and you will produce this sound.

Listening Exercise 3.

Listen to and repeat these words containing خ :

خاب　　بَخيل　　باخ　　بَخت　　تَختي　　فَرَخ

Writing

ـخ	ـخـ	خـ	خ

خ is a connector, and its shapes are written exactly as those of ج and ح, except that it takes one dot above. Practice writing initial خ in the word خاب , saying it as you write:

خاب

Practice writing and pronouncing medial خ in بَخت (*luck*):

بَخت

Now practice final خ by copying the word بَخ :

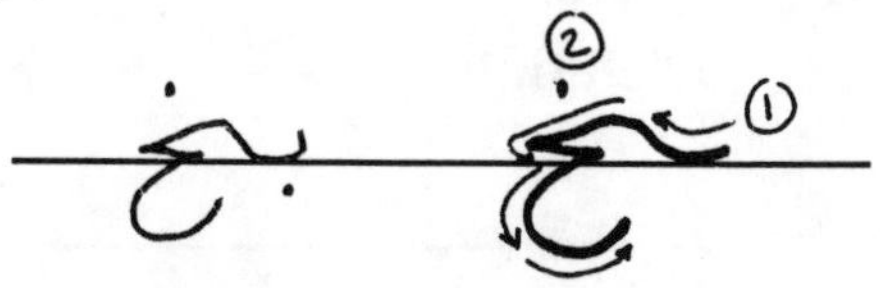

Drill 3.

You will hear twelve words, each containing ج , ح , or خ . Write the letter you hear in each word:

1. ______ 5. ______ 9. ______
2. ______ 6. ______ 10. ______
3. ______ 7. ______ 11. ______
4. ______ 8. ______ 12. ______

Drill 4.

Connect the following letters to form words, then listen to the words on tape and mark in the short vowels where you hear them:

1. ______________________ = خ + ا + ب + ت
2. ______________________ = ح + ج + ا + ب
3. ______________________ = ح + ب + ي + ب
4. ______________________ = ت + خ + و + ت
5. ______________________ = ت + ج + و + ب
6. ______________________ = ب + ح + و + ث
7. ______________________ = ت + ب + و + ح + ي
8. ______________________ = ح + ج + ب + ت

Drill 5.
Dictation.

1. ____________ 4. ____________

2. ____________ 5. ____________

3. ____________ 6. ____________

Drill 6.
Read these words aloud (read across from right to left). Pay special attention to vowel length and the sounds ح and خ .

حَج	جابي	تَحتاج
حاج	جُبَب	حِجاب
حُب	خاب	جابَت
بُح	تُجاب	باحِث
خوجا	تُخوت	جيبوتي

ـْ "sukuun"

This symbol is a pronunciation marker that indicates the absence of a short vowel. So far, you have learned to use fatHa, Damma, and kasra over consonants to indicate the short vowels, and consonants not followed by a vowel have been left "blank." In fully vowelled texts, however, all consonants have at least one marking, even if no vowel occurs, because there is a special symbol to indicate the absence of a vowel. This symbol is called *sukuun* (meaning *silence*).

Listening Exercise 4.
Listen and repeat:

تَحْت بَخْت تَحْجُب تَخْت تَحْتاج

WRITING

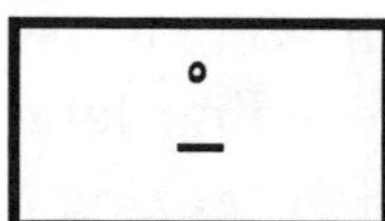

Like the short vowel symbols, the sukuun is rarely used in unvowelled or partially vowelled texts. When it is written, it appears as a small open circle above a letter not followed by a vowel. In writing sukuun, make sure to draw a circle and not a Damma or a dot. Practice writing the sukuun by copying the examples:

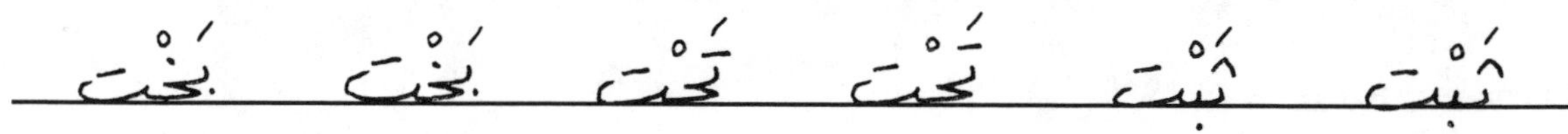

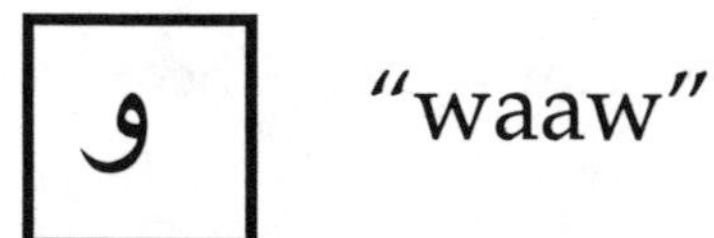

"waaw"

In Unit One, you learned that و represents the long vowel sound "oo." It also has a second function, related to the first one: when preceded or followed by a long or short vowel, this letter is pronounced *w* as in *well*, or as in the name of the letter: واو "waaw." To understand how these two sounds are related, pronounce *oo* and hold it *oooooooooo* then go right into *a*. You will hear a *w* sound connecting the two vowels. At the beginning of a word, و will always be pronounced *w*, because Arabic words cannot begin with a vowel. **Remember:** any vowel, short or long, preceding or following و turns it into a consonant.

LISTENING EXERCISE 5.

Listen to and repeat the following words containing و as a consonant:

وَثَبَ　　واجِب　　زَواج　　جَواب　　حِوار　　خاوي

Just as *w* occurs in diphthongs[1] in English, so does و in Arabic. However, Arabic has only one diphthong with و , which is ـَو (و preceded by a fatHa). The sound of this combination is similar to the sound spelled *ow* in *mow* or *know* (**not** the same as *ow* in *crowd*). **Do not** confuse pronunciation and spelling; there are several different diphthong sounds in English and their spellings overlap.

[1]A diphthong is a combination of vowel and semi-vowel sounds, such as *ow* in *cow, ow* in *mow,*or *aw* in *saw*.

In unvowelled texts, this diphthong is usually not indicated; however, it may be indicated by a fatHa on the preceding letter **or** a sukuun on و **or both**. The following are three different ways of vocalizing the word خوخ (*peach*):

خَوخ = خوْخ = خَوْخ

The sukuun alone can indicate this sound because it can only occur on consonants, so if you see ـوْ , you know that the letter is functioning as a consonant, and that a vowel precedes it. In such a case, the vowel must be a fatHa .

Listening Exercise 6.

Listen to the sound of the diphthong ـَو in the following words and repeat:

ثَوب زَوج تَوبيخ خَوخ حَول خَوف

Drill 7.

Copy the following words, sounding them out as you write. Check your pronunciation against the tape.

خاب خَوخ تَبويب تَحتاج ثَواب زَوج

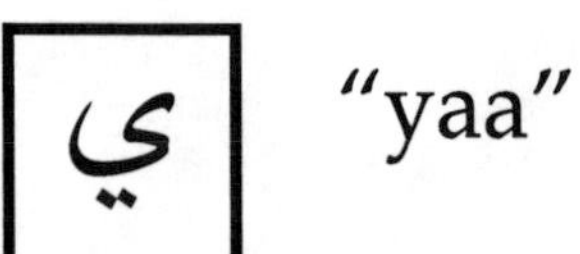

"yaa"

The long vowel ي also functions as a consonant at the beginning of a word, or when preceded or followed by a vowel: it is pronounced like *y* in *yes*. Say *eeeeeee* and go right into *a* and you will hear yourself say *y*.

Listening Exercise 7.

Practice reading the following words containing the consonant ي with the tape:

بُيوت ثِياب جُيوب يَجِب يَثوب

When ي is preceded by a fatHa and followed by sukuun, it forms a diphthong that is pronounced like *ay* as in *say*, or, if near emphatic letters, like *i* in *ice*. The sukuun alone may be written on ي to indicate this diphthong, or the fatHa may be used, or both sukuun and fatHa. The following are three different ways of vocalizing the word بيت (*house*):

بَيْت = بيْت = بَيت

The sukuun alone can indicate these diphthongs because it can only occur on consonants, so if you see ـيْـ , you know that the letter is functioning as a consonant, and that a vowel precedes it. In this case, the vowel must be a fatHa .

Listening Exercise 8.

Listen to the sound of the diphthong ـيَـ in these words and repeat:

حَيث   خَير   جَيب   بَيت   بَين

Drill 8.

Copy the following words while sounding them out. Then check your pronunciation against the tape.

ثِياب   حَياتي   جُيوبي   بُيوت   يَحْجُب

____

____

Drill 9.

Read these words aloud (across from right to left):

جَواب   جَوابات   بَحْث   واجِبات

حَبيبي   حَبيبَتي   ثَواب   جَيْبي

يَجِب   حَيْث   بُيوت   تُجيبي

وُجوب   خابَ   بَيتي   جُيوب

جُثَث   تَبوحي   يَخْت   ثِيابي

Drill 10.

Connect the following letters to form words. Then listen to the words on tape and write in all the short vowels that you hear.

1. ____________________ = ج + ا + ب + ت
2. ____________________ = ح + ج + ب
3. ____________________ = خ + و + خ
4. ____________________ = ث + ي + ا + ب + ي
5. ____________________ = ج + ي + ب + و + ت + ي
6. ____________________ = ح + ب + ي + ب + ت + ي
7. ____________________ = ب + ح + و + ث
8. ____________________ = و + ا + ج + ب + ا + ت
9. ____________________ = ب + ي + و + ت
10. ____________________ = ج + ي + و + ب

Drill 11.

Dictation.

1. ____________________
2. ____________________
3. ____________________
4. ____________________
5. ____________________
6. ____________________

Drill 12.

Read the following advertisements:

1. PEUGEOT | بيجو

2.

3.

من جريدة الشرق الاوسط، ١٩٩٣

Culture الثقافة

Video

Watch Scenes 3, 4, and 5 on the video tape with your teacher.

Meeting and Greeting People

In Arab culture, it is considered rude not to say good morning, good evening, or hello to someone you know, even casually, the first time you see them each day. In addition, when you enter a room, you should greet people already there whether or not you know them.

In social situations, it is polite to shake hands upon meeting or greeting another person, especially someone of the same gender. Some people do not shake hands with members of the opposite sex; this is a matter of personal preference or religious belief. Close friends of the same gender often greet each other by kissing on both cheeks.

الوحدة الثالثة
UNIT THREE

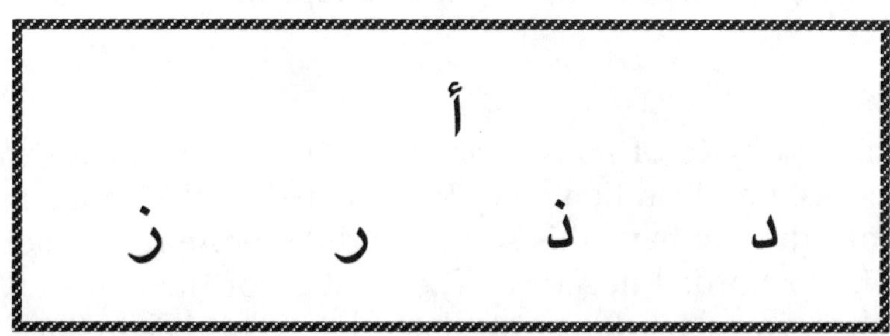

In this unit you will learn about the second function of alif and the next four consonants in the alphabet.

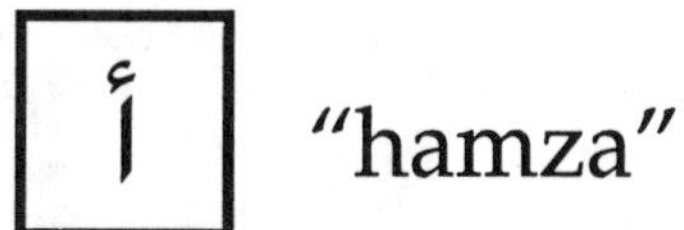

In Unit Two you saw that و and ي sometimes function as consonants. Remember that they always function as consonants at the beginning of a word. The letter ا can also represent a consonant sound when it occurs at the beginning of a word. The consonant that it stands for is called *hamza;* you can see its shape on top of the alif in the box above. Initial hamza is **often, but not always,** written on top of the alif that represents it. Thus, it may appear as ا **or** as أ . **Remember**: initial alif is always a seat for hamza, never a long vowel.

Hamza is a sound you make in English all the time—every time you say a word that begins with a vowel, in fact—but you do not recognize it as a consonant because English has no letter for it.[1] Say *uh-oh* several times and pay attention to the sound you make in between the two syllables. You make the same sound when you pronounce any word that begins with a vowel, such as *our, if, it, I, on, up*. Say these out loud, and pay attention to the "catch" in your throat as you pronounce the first vowel. This sound is not written out in English, which treats these words as if they began with a vowel. In Arabic, however, this sound is considered to be a consonant. **Remember:** in Arabic, no word or syllable begins with a vowel, short or long. The consonant hamza must precede all initial vowel sounds.

---

[1]In linguistic terminology, this sound is called "glottal stop."

Hamza occurs not only at the beginning, but also in the middle or at the end of a word. Practice hamza by saying *uh-oh* until you can say it effortlessly, then do the following listening exercises on tape.

Listening Exercise 1.

Practice saying hamza by listening to and repeating these words:

أَخَوات　　أَب　　سَبَأ　　تَأتَأ　　بَأس

Hamza has no place of its own in the alphabet, for historical reasons that involve Quranic spelling. Tradition holds that the dialect of Mecca which the Prophet Muhammed spoke did not have this sound, and therefore it was not written when the Quran was first recorded in script. The symbol for the hamza was developed, along with the short vowel markings, at a later date. This is why hamza is treated as a pronunciation marker rather than as part of the alphabet, and why hamza has several different "spellings," depending on its position in the word and the vowel sounds surrounding it. In this unit you will learn the two most common spellings, أ and ء .

At the beginning of a word hamza is represented by alif, either ا or أ . The alif is considered to be the "seat" of the hamza in this case.

Listening Exercise 2.

Listen to initial hamza in following words on tape and repeat:

أَب　　أَتَت　　أَخ　　أَخَوات　　أَثاث

The words above all begin with hamza followed by the vowel fatHa. In addition, the other short vowels may appear in this position; that is, أ serves as a seat for Damma and kasra as well. Note that when the initial vowel is **kasra**, the hamza is often written **underneath** the alif, as in: إِثبات . **Remember:** while ا and أ **can** carry the kasra, إ **always** indicates a kasra vowel.

Listening Exercise 3.

Listen to initial hamza with vowels Damma and kasra and repeat:

إِبْحار　　أُخْت　　إِثْبات　　أُخْرِجَ　　إِخْبار　　أُثبِتَ

In fully vocalized texts, the short vowel will be marked. In unvocalized texts, you will see only the consonant skeleton. To read an unvocalized word correctly, you need to know it, or make an educated guess based on knowledge of Arabic word patterns (this will become clear later on). Learn to associate the pronunciation of each new vocabulary item with its consonant frame, the same way you associate certain pronunciations in English with certain spellings (think of *neighbor* and *weigh*, *taught* and *caught*). In your native language, you read by word, not by syllable; it is important to develop this same skill in Arabic.

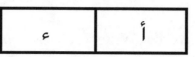

Writing

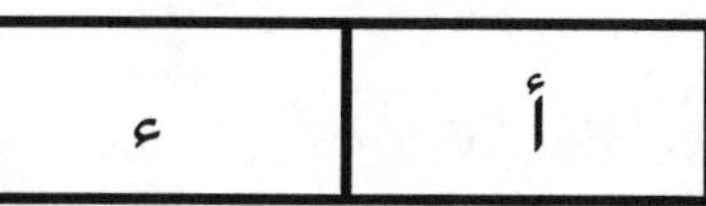

The actual shape of the hamza, shown above, is a small c-shape that continues into a line on the bottom. At the beginning of a word, it is always written on alif, or the alif alone may represent it. When it occurs in the middle of a word, it may be written on any one of the long vowels like this: أ , ؤ , or ئ , depending on the surrounding vowels. You will learn these other spellings of hamza later. When hamza occurs after a long vowel at the end of a word, it is usually written on the line, without a seat, in which case it is somewhat larger in size. Following the arrows, copy and practice the shape of independent hamza:

ء ء

Listening Exercise 4.

The names of many letters of the alphabet end in hamza. Listen to and repeat the names of letters you have learned:

باء تاء ثاء حاء خاء

Practice writing final hamza by copying these names, pronouncing them as you write:

Now practice writing the initial hamza on alif by copying the words أخ (*brother*), أُخت (*sister*), and إثبات (*proof*):

أَخ أُخت إِثبات

Drill 1.

You will hear twelve words. Write ء for each word in which you hear it:

1. _____ 5. _____ 9. _____

2. _____ 6. _____ 10. _____

3. _____ 7. _____ 11. _____

4. _____ 8. _____ 12. _____

Drill 2.

Dictation.

1. _______________ 4. _______________

2. _______________ 5. _______________

3. _______________ 6. _______________

د "daal"

This consonant is pronounced like a clear, frontal *d* in English, as in the word *dentist* (**not** like the *d* sound in *puddle*). Pay particular attention to your pronunciation of medial and final د , and to the surrounding vowel sounds, which should be frontal in quality (remember *a* in *bad* and *e* in *bet*).

Listening Exercise 5.

Listen to and repeat the following words containing د :

دَجاج　　خُدود　　حُدود　　جَديد　　أَدَب　　أَحْداث

Writing

ـد	ـد	د	د

The letter د is a nonconnector, so it does not connect to any letter that follows it. To write initial د , begin well above the line, and slant down as shown below. Just before hitting the line, angle sharply and finish along the line into a tiny hook. In handwriting, the exact shape and slant of this letter vary slightly according to individual style; the important components are the acute angle and that the body remain above the line. Copy, following the arrows:

د ①د

To write د when it is connected to a previous letter in medial or final position, begin from the connecting segment, draw the top half of the letter from the line up, then trace your line back down, make a sharp angle as before, and finish. When connected from the previous letter, the top half of the angle tends to have a slightly different shape because of the connecting segment. Copy:

ـد ①ـد

Now practice by copying the words دَجاج (*chicken*) and جَديد (*new*):

ذ "dhaal"

In Unit One, you learned to distinguish between the sound *th* in *three*, represented in Arabic by the letter ث, and the sound *th* in the word *other*. The letter ذ represents the *other* sound (pun intended—remember it this way!).

Listening Exercise 6.

Listen and repeat:

ذُباب   ذات   بَذَر   خُذ   حَذارِ   تَذبْذُب

Writing

ذ	ذ	ـذ	ـذ

The letter ذ is a nonconnector, and is written just like د, except that it takes a single dot above. Like د, it does not connect to a following letter, and has only two forms, initial/independent and medial/final. Practice the initial/independent form by copying ذُباب (*flies*):

ذُباب

Practice writing the medial/final form by copying خُذ (*take!*):

خُذ

Now copy and read aloud these words:

ذات   ذَوات   جَذّاب   أَخَذ

Drill 3.

You will hear twelve words on tape, each containing either ذ or ث . Circle the sound you hear in each word:

1.	ث	ذ	5.	ث	ذ	9.	ث	ذ
2.	ث	ذ	6.	ث	ذ	10.	ث	ذ
3.	ث	ذ	7.	ث	ذ	11.	ث	ذ
4.	ث	ذ	8.	ث	ذ	12.	ث	ذ

Drill 4.

Read the following words aloud, paying particular attention to the pronunciation of ث and ذ .

1.	ذابَ	5.	ثَواب
2.	ثابَ	6.	ذَوات
3.	ذُباب	7.	جُثَث
4.	ثَبات	8.	جاذِب

Drill 5.

You will hear eight words. For each, write the missing letter in the blank:

1.	تَـــوب	5.	ـــوبي
2.	خُـوَ ـــ	6.	جَـــب
3.	ـــات	7.	أـــا ـــ
4.	أـــواب	8.	خُـــي

ر "raa"

This is the name of the Arabic *r*. It is a flap, like the Spanish or Italian *r*. You already know how to make this sound: it is the sound American English speakers make saying *gotta* as in *gotta go*. Say *gotta* several times in a row very quickly and pay attention to what your tongue is doing. You should feel it flapping against the roof of your mouth behind your teeth. Now pronounce the sound alone. Another good exercise is to practice making a whirring sound: *rrrrrrrrrr*. Do these exercises daily until you have mastered this sound.

Listening Exercise 7.

Practice saying ر by repeating the following words. Notice that ر usually deepens the quality of alif and fatHa so that they sound deep like *a* in *father* .

رَباب   رُدود   خَراج   تَبْرير   جار   وُرود

Writing

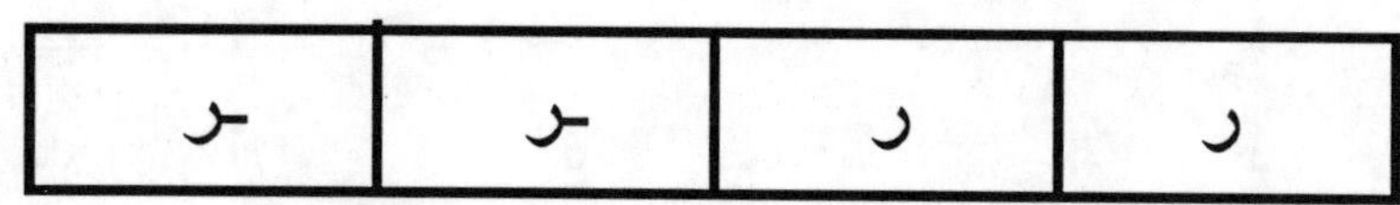

This letter is a nonconnector, and is written almost entirely below the line. You will see that the exact angle and shape of the ر vary somewhat in handwriting and print styles, but it may be distinguished from د by its wide angle and its long tail that dips well below the line (remember that د rests on the line). To write initial ر , begin on the line and curve downwards below it. Imitate the shape in the example:

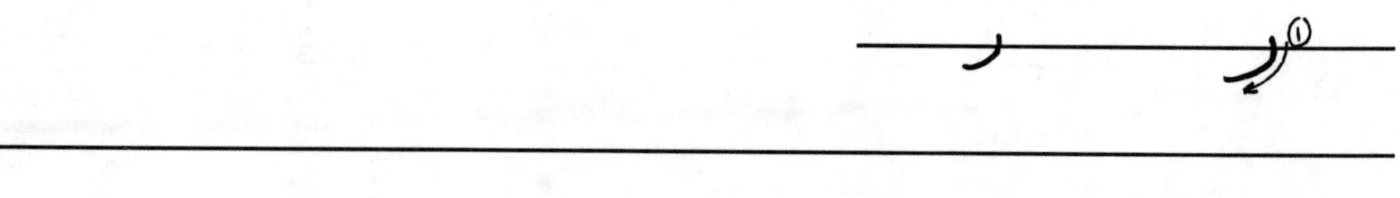

To write ـر connected from a previous letter, start from the connecting segment on the line, then curve down. Copy:

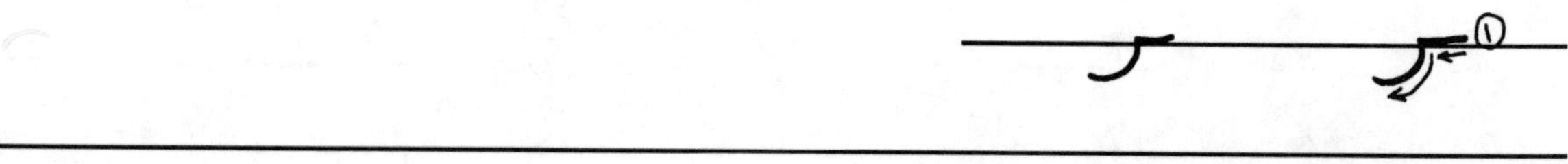

Drill 6.

Copy and sound out the following words:

بَرْد   خُروج   راجي   بارِد   تَحرير   جورج   يَروح

ز

"zaay"

This consonant corresponds to the English sound *z* in *zebra*.

Listening Exercise 8.

Read the following words containing the sound ز along with the tape:

تَزيد جَواز يَزور زُجاج أحْزاب زَوْج

Writing

ـز	ـز	ز	ز

The letter ز is a nonconnector, and has the same shape as ر , except that it takes one dot above. Using the same techniques you used for ر , practice writing and reading initial/independent ز by copying:

ز ز

Copy ـز in medial and final position:

ـز ـز

Now copy and sound out the following female and male names:

♀ وَداد بُدور رَباب تاج رَجاء

♂ زَيد بَدر زايِد حارِث ديب

___

___

Drill 7. 📼

Connect the letters to form words, then listen to them on tape and write in the short vowels as you hear them:

1. ____________ = ر + ذ + ا + ذ
2. ____________ = خ + ا + د + ر
3. ____________ = ز + ر + د
4. ____________ = ح + ر + و + ب
5. ____________ = ر + ج + ا + ء
6. ____________ = ب + ح + ا + ر
7. ____________ = أ + ز + و + ا + ج
8. ____________ = ح + د + و + د
9. ____________ = ر + د + و + د
10. ____________ = ت + ح + ذ + ي + ر
11. ____________ = أ + د + و + ا + ر
12. ____________ = ي + خ + ر + ج
13. ____________ = ت + ج + ا + ر + ب
14. ____________ = ذ + ب + ح + ت

Drill 8.

Dictation.

1. ______________	6. ______________
2. ______________	7. ______________
3. ______________	8. ______________
4. ______________	9. ______________
5. ______________	10. ______________

Drill 9.

Read the following words aloud:

دار	واحِد	حِزْب	وَرْد
زُيوت	أزرار	بَيْروت	إِخْبار
زُجاج	أبي	يَجري	تَأثير
تَثاءَبَ	خَرَز	ذَوات	تَحْذير
دَجاج	بازار	بير زَيْت	بارِد
أُخْت	حُروب	زَيْت	وَحيد
جَرير	أحْزاب	أخَوات	ثَأر
وُزَراء	ثَوْر	يَدور	بَحْري

Drill 10.

Read aloud the following advertisements:

1.

من جريدة الشرق الاوسط، ١٩٩٣

2.

من جريدة الشرق الاوسط، ١٩٩٣

3.

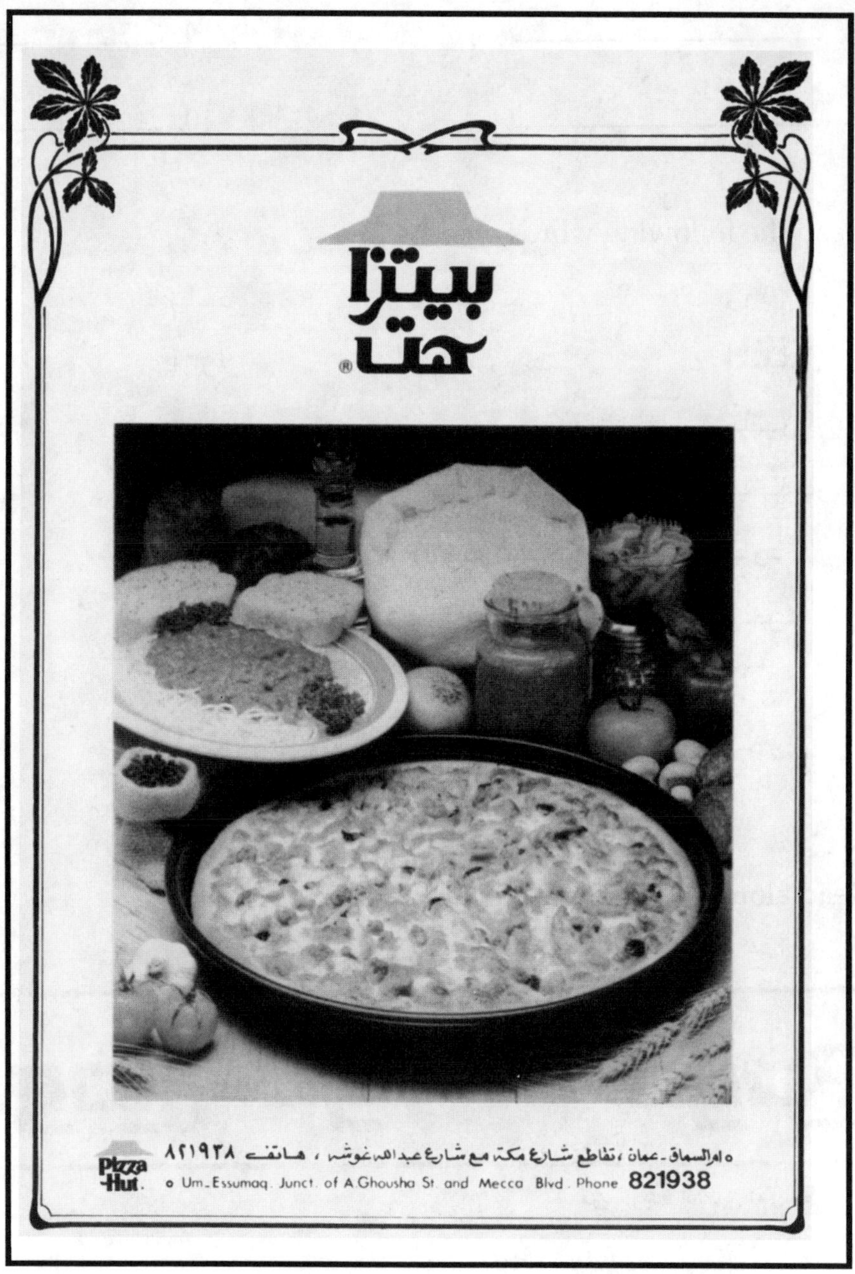

من "دليلك في عمان"، مارس (آذار) ١٩٩٤

CULTURE الثقافة

VIDEO

Watch Scenes 6 and 7 on video with your teacher.

AL-HAMDU LILLAAH

Literally *Praise be to God*, or *Thank God*, this is one of the most widely used phrases in Arabic by people of all religious backgrounds. Its most common uses are (a) in response to *How are you?* whether or not one is well, because God is to be thanked at all times, (b) upon finishing a meal, to signal that one has had enough, and (c) upon successfully completing a task or learning of a positive outcome.

ARABIC DIALECTS

Every language has some differences between its written and spoken forms. Pronunciation usually varies from region to region, and some vocabulary differs; occasionally there are differences in grammar as well. For example, *I dunno* is rarely written, except for special effect, and *I do not know* is rarely used in speech. *Hoagie, submarine, sub, wedge,* and *hero* all refer to the same sandwich, and American southerners often distinguish between singular *you* and plural *y'all*. Americans, Britons, and Australians learn to understand each other's accents merely by being exposed to them.

The Arabic language also varies in these ways, although the differences are sometimes greater than those found among varieties of English. Names for the different varieties of Arabic include Modern Standard, colloquial, and Classical Arabic. In this book, the terms "formal" and "spoken" will be used to differentiate between written and spoken forms of the language. All varieties of Arabic share the same basic grammar and most vocabulary. The greatest differences lie in the areas of accent and daily-life vocabulary. For some examples of these differences, listen to a few expressions from four regions:

	Cairo	Beirut	Fez	Baghdad
Good morning!	*SabaaH ilkheer*	*SabaaH lkheer*	*SbaH lkher*	*SbaaH lkheer*
How are you?	*izzayyak? (m)*	*kiifak? (m)*	*laa baas?*	*shloonak? (m)*
What's your name?	*ismak ee? (m)*	*shuu ismak? (m)*	*shnu smiitk?*	*sh- ismak? (m)*
Milk	*laban*	*Haliib*	*Hliib*	*Haliib*

As you can see and hear, the accents are different and some of the expressions differ, although they are all related to formal Arabic. Notice, for example, the consistent use of *ak* or *k* for *your*. The more formal Arabic you know, the easier it is to recognize the dialect forms that are derived from it.

In this book, you will concentrate on learning to read and write modern formal Arabic. You will also learn to speak in formal Arabic, while being introduced to common expressions used in daily life in Egypt through the video tape. The Egyptian dialect is widely understood throughout the Arab world, thanks to the popularity of Egyptian films and television shows. You will notice some differences in pronunciation and vocabulary between formal Arabic and the Egyptian dialect; for example, it was noted above—and you can hear on the tape—that the letter ج is pronounced *g* in Egypt. You will learn other differences as they arise.

To be fluent in Arabic, you must have control of both the formal and colloquial registers. It is quite natural to mix the two, and this is a skill that native speakers develop over the course of their formal and social education. You will develop this skill too; after all, you already shift from one level to another naturally in your native language. The more Arabic you learn, the easier it will become to recognize, understand and use the different varieties of Arabic.

الوحدة الرابعة
UNIT FOUR

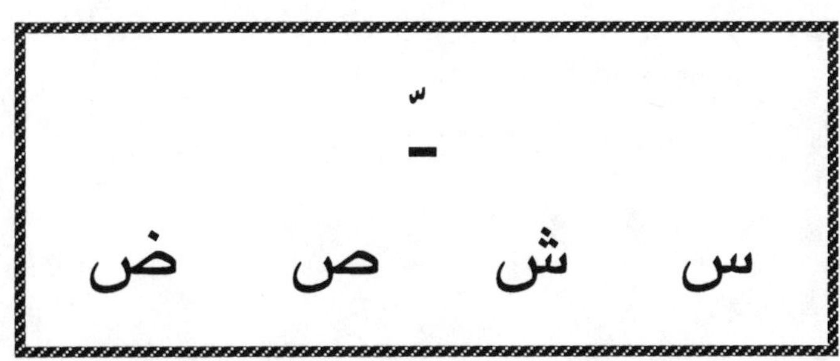

In this unit, you will learn the symbol for doubling consonants, and the next four letters of the alphabet in sequence.

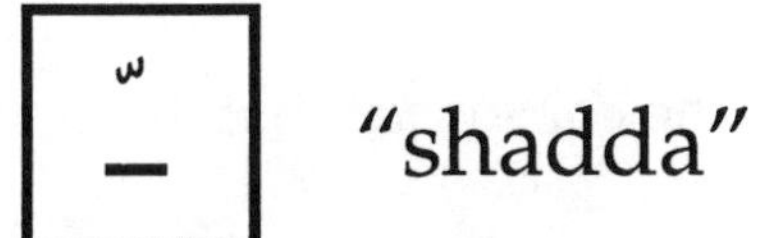

This symbol, called *shadda*, is a pronunciation marker whose function is to double the length of a consonant in pronunciation. **Do not** associate the shadda with two identical, consecutive consonants in English, as in the word *little*; in English, doubling is merely a spelling convention that may affect the vowel sound, but not the pronunciation of the consonant itself. In Arabic, doubling **changes the pronunciation** of the consonant over which it is written, and **affects the meaning** of any word in which it occurs. Like other vocalization marks, shadda is usually omitted in unvowelled texts, except where ambiguity might arise without it. In general, the reader is expected to know which words take shadda, and to use context, if necessary, to guess.

Any consonant may be doubled as long as it does not begin a word. The difference between a single consonant and a doubled one is one of length: a doubled consonant is pronounced and held for **twice as long** as a single one. This is easy to do with fluid sounds, like ث , ذ , ج , ح , خ , ر , and ز . To double the sounds ب , ت , and د , you must begin to say them and pause in the middle of pronouncing them for a second. Practice this by doing the following exercise.

Listening Exercise 1.

Listen to the difference in pronunciation between the first and second word in each pair and repeat:

تَجِدُ /تَجِدُّ　　دَرَسَ /دَرَّسَ　　حاجة /حاجّة　　شاب/شابّ　　خَرَجَ / خَرَّجَ

Drill 1.

You will hear twelve words. Mark **X** if you hear a shadda:

1. ____ 5. ____ 9. ____

2. ____ 6. ____ 10. ____

3. ____ 7. ____ 11. ____

4. ____ 8. ____ 12. ____

Writing

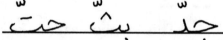

Shadda is written like a tiny, rounded **ɯ** on top of the consonant that it doubles. Practice by copying the examples:

جدّ بشّ حتّ

Now practice writing and reading shadda in these words:

يَتَزَوَّج يُدَرِّب حاجّ خَبّاز جَبّور

When kasra and shadda occur together on the same consonant, they may be written in their normal positions, as in (1) below, **or** the kasra may be written just below the shadda, above the letter, as in (2):

(1) يُدَرِّب = (2) يُدَرِّب

You will see both variants, so learn to recognize them.

Be aware that you must listen carefully to distinguish between a long vowel sound and a shadda in the middle of a word. Practice listening for and pronouncing this difference in the next exercise.

Listening Exercise 2.

Compare the following pairs of words, the first of which has a long vowel and the second a shadda. Listen and repeat out loud several times:

راجَع / رَجَّع   جاوَز / جَوَّز   تَزاوَج / تَزَوَّج   دارِس / دَرِّس   دوري / دُرّي

Drill 2.

You will hear twelve words, each containing either a shadda or a long vowel. Indicate which words contain long vowels, and which shadda by writing either the long vowel you hear or shadda:

1. _____ 5. _____ 9. _____

2. _____ 6. _____ 10. _____

3. _____ 7. _____ 11. _____

4. _____ 8. _____ 12. _____

Drill 3.

Dictation.

1. _______________ 4. _______________

2. _______________ 5. _______________

3. _______________ 6. _______________

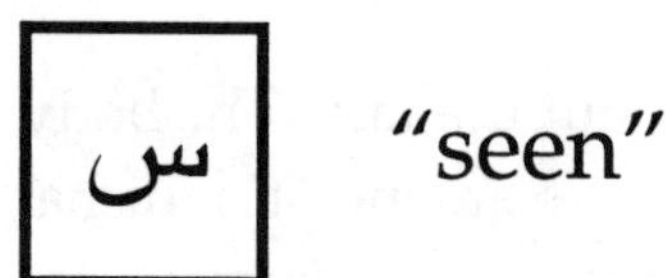

"seen"

Seen is the name of the Arabic letter corresponding to English *s* as in the word *seen*. Be careful not to confuse pronunciation and spelling in this case, for *s* is used to spell several different sounds in English, such as *z* as in *easy* or *zh* as in *treasure* . س is a frontal consonant, which means that you must pay attention to the quality of the vowels surrounding it. In particular, when alif and fatHa occur before or after س , they are frontal, as in *bad* and *bet*.

Listening Exercise 3.

Repeat, paying particular attention to the vowel sounds:

سادات   مَساء   بَسّ   سُبات   وَسْواس   حَسَد

Writing

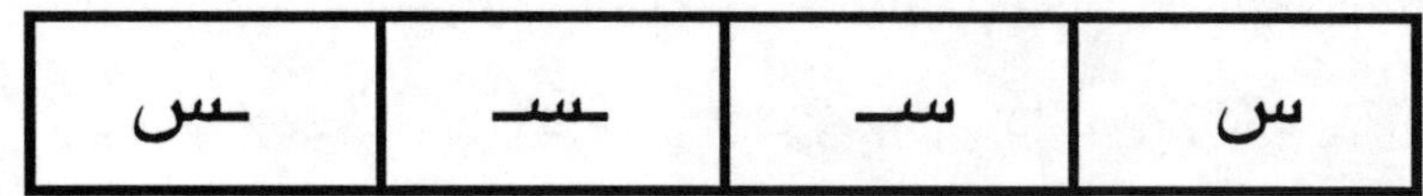

س is a connecting letter that is distinguished in print by its three "teeth." In handwriting, however, س is usually written without its teeth, as a long straight line. In either case, it takes a tail when written independently or in final position. Compare the printed and handwritten forms of the following:

سبب   حسب   درس

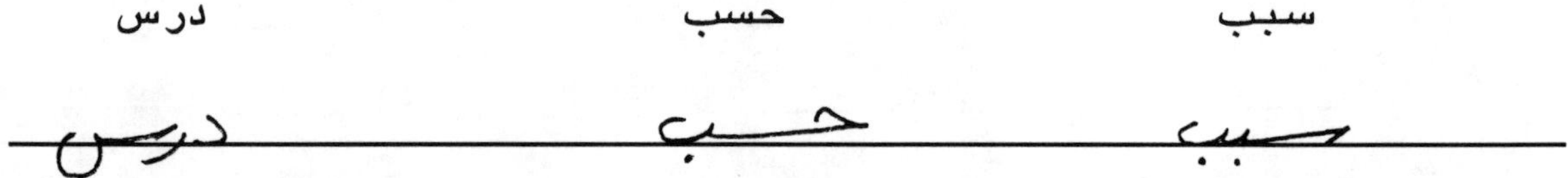

You will quickly become accustomed to reading س with its teeth in print. **Learn to write it without them.** To write independent س , begin on the line and draw a very small hook, just enough to indicate the beginning of a letter. Continue into the long, flat body, then dip below the line into the tail, **making sure that it comes all the way back up to the line in a full semicircle.** Copy:

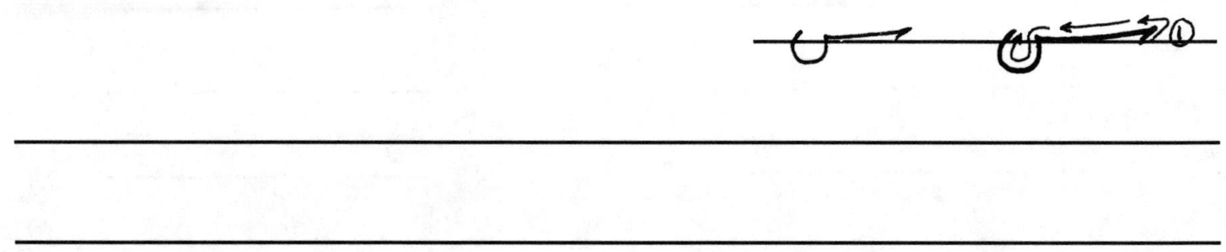

Initial سـ is written just like independent س but without the tail. The body of connected ـسـ merges into the connecting segment so that the two are indistinguishable, so make sure to **lengthen** the body of the letter. Copy the word سَبَب (*reason*):

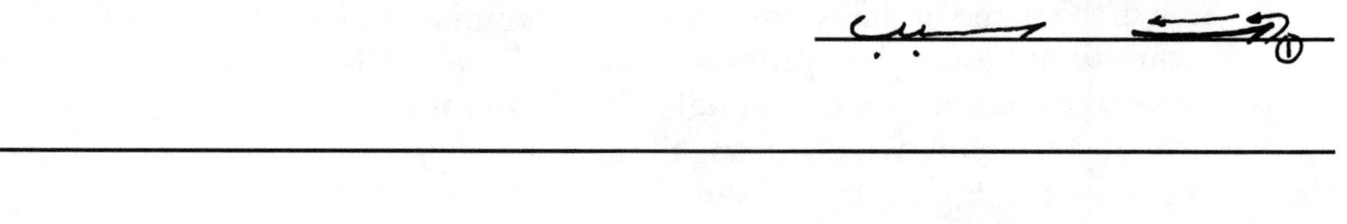

When ـسـ is connected from a previous letter in medial or final position, the connecting segment and the body of the letter are indistinguishable and **there is no hook on the beginning**, so that it looks like this: ———. The body of this toothless س must be long enough to distinguishing it from a connecting segment. **Remember** when reading handwriting that a long flat line like this: ——— represents ـسـ. Copy this medial handwritten form in the word حِساب (*arithmetic*):

Final ـس is written with its tail, which **must come all the way back up to the line** (lest it be mistaken for ـر). Copy final ـس in the colloquial word بَسّ (*that's all, enough*):

Drill 4.

Dictation.

1. ____________ 4. ____________

2. ____________ 5. ____________

3. ____________ 6. ____________

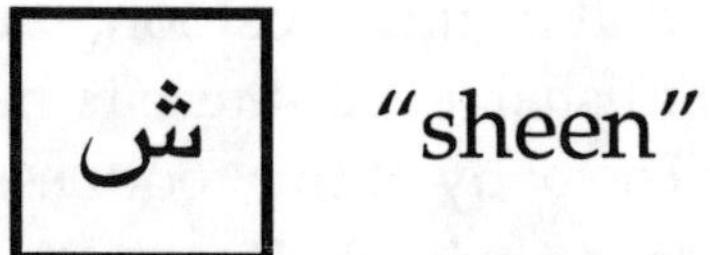

This letter corresponds to the sound *sh* in *shoe*.

Listening Exercise 4.

Listen to ش in these words and repeat:

شَمْس　　شِبْر　　بَشير　　باشا　　حَشيش　　رَشّاش

Writing

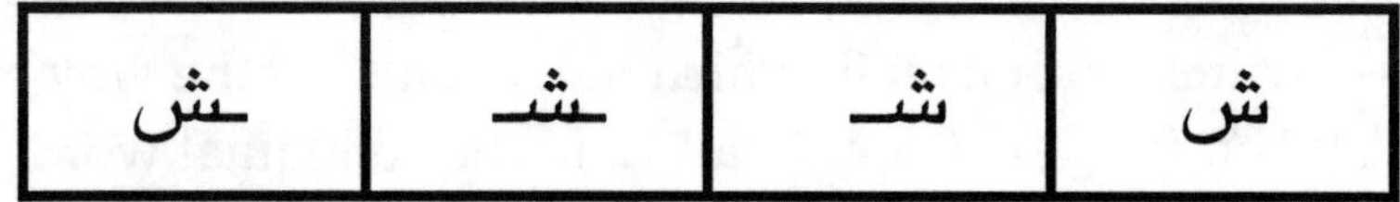

The letter ش is a connector, and its shapes match those of س , except that this letter takes three dots above. In handwriting, ش is written without it teeth (like س) and the three dots are connected in a caret (just like those of ث).

Practice writing independent ش by copying the example:

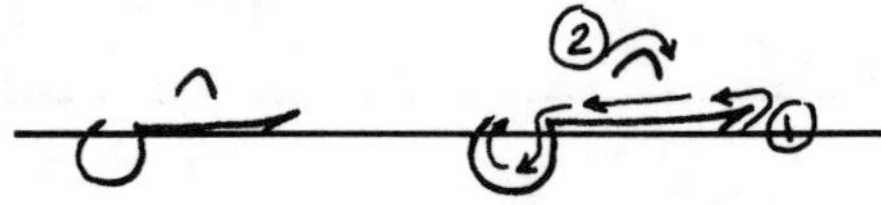

Now practice initial شـ by copying شَيْخ (*shaykh*):

Copy medial and final ـشـ ـش in حَشيش (*grass*):

Now copy and sound out the following names:

♀ سَحَر سَراب ثُرَيّا ريتّا

♂ سَيِّد بَشير رَشيد وَحيد

Drill 5.

Dictation.

1. ______________
2. ______________
3. ______________
4. ______________
5. ______________
6. ______________

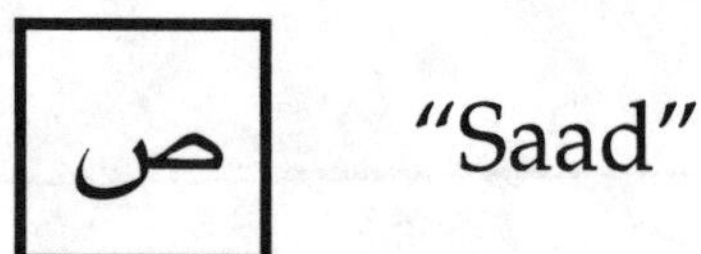

ص "Saad"

This letter represents the emphatic counterpart of س . Pronounce س aloud, and note the position of your tongue. It should be toward the front of the mouth and high, close to the roof. Now, starting at the back of your teeth, move your tongue back along the roof of your mouth. You will find a bony ridge just behind the teeth, before the upward curve of the roof. Put your tongue against this ridge. The rest of your tongue will drop lower inside your mouth. The emphatic or velarized consonants in Arabic are pronounced by placing the tip of your tongue in this spot and dropping the rest of the tongue as low as you can. **Remember:** this and other emphatic consonants deepen the sound of surrounding vowels, most noticeably alif and fatHa, which sound like *a* in *father* and *u* in *but*. Pay attention to the sound of all vowels near these emphatic letters, because **the quality of the vowels gives the clearest indication of emphatic consonants.**

Listening Exercise 5.

Listen to these words containing ص and repeat, paying particular attention to the surrounding vowels:

صاد   صار   صَباح   صُوَر   حِصّة   لُصوص

Writing

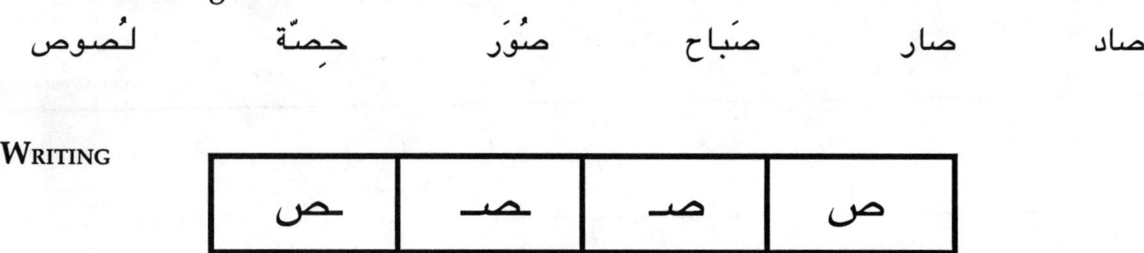

The letter ص is a connector, and it retains the same basic shape in both print and handwriting. There are two essential points to keep in mind when writing ص : (a) the loop must be big and oval-shaped, and (b) there must be a small "tooth" after the loop. To write independent ص , start on the line and make a big loop up and back to your right, then swing down and close it. Without stopping, make the tooth and then drop well below the line to make the tail. The tail of ص is the same shape as that of س and **must come all the way back up to the line**. Copy:

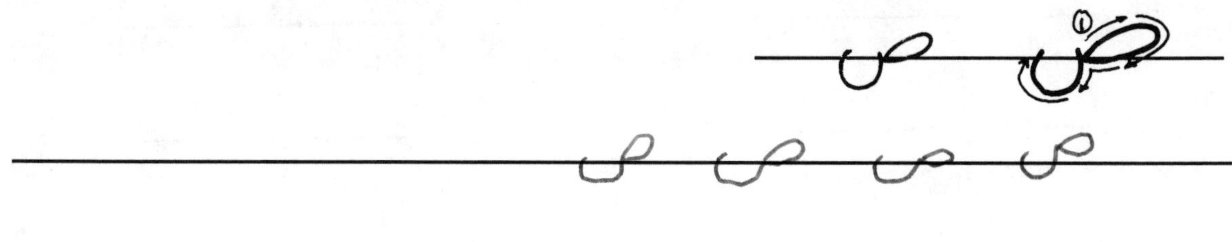

Initial صـ is written the same way, without the tail. After making the tooth, continue on to the connecting segment. Copy صَباح (*morning*):

صباح

To write ـصـ connected from a previous letter, draw the connecting segment to the starting point of the loop, the same point at which you started in initial position, then follow the same steps as above. Copy, following the arrows:

ـصـ

Practice by copying the word تَصْوير (*photography*):

تَصْوير

Final ـص is connected the same way as medial ـصـ and ends with a final tail the same shape as the tail of س . Practice by copying شَخْص (*person*):

شَخْص

Listening Exercise 6. 📼

Listen to and repeat the following pairs of words contrasting س and ص . Notice that the emphatic quality of ص deepens the sound of surrounding vowels. Listening to vowel quality is the easiest way to distinguish between س and ص.

أصبَح / أسبَح   صاح / ساح   صين / سين   صُوَر / سُوَر   حَصَد / حَسَد

Drill 6. 📼

Read these words aloud with the tape, paying attention to the difference between س and ص:

1. (a) سارَ (b) صارَ
2. (a) باس (b) باص
3. (a) أسير (b) أصير
4. (a) سَبْر (b) صَبْر
5. (a) خَسّ (b) خَصّ
6. (a) سَدَّت (b) صَدَّت

Drill 7. 📼

Listen to the words on tape and write the letter you hear in the blank. Remember to listen for vowel quality to help you distinguish between س and ص .

1. ــــابِح
2. بَــــير
3. بَــــ
4. تَــــدُر
5. يَدرُ ــــا
6. ــــوْتي
7. أ ــــبَح
8. حَــــد

Drill 8. 📼

You will hear twelve words; each has either س or ص . Write the letter that corresponds to the sound you hear:

1. _____ 5. _____ 9. _____
2. _____ 6. _____ 10. _____
3. _____ 7. _____ 11. _____
4. _____ 8. _____ 12. _____

Drill 9.

Dictation.

1. ____________ 4. ____________

2. ____________ 5. ____________

3. ____________ 6. ____________

"Daad"

This letter represents the emphatic counterpart of د . To pronounce ض , place your tongue in the same position as you did to say ص and try to say د ; the result will be ض . Remember that ض is an emphatic consonant that deepens the quality of surrounding vowels, especially alif and fatHa.

Listening Exercise 7.

Listen to ض in these words and repeat:

ضاد ضَباب خَضَّ حَضَر رِياض

Writing

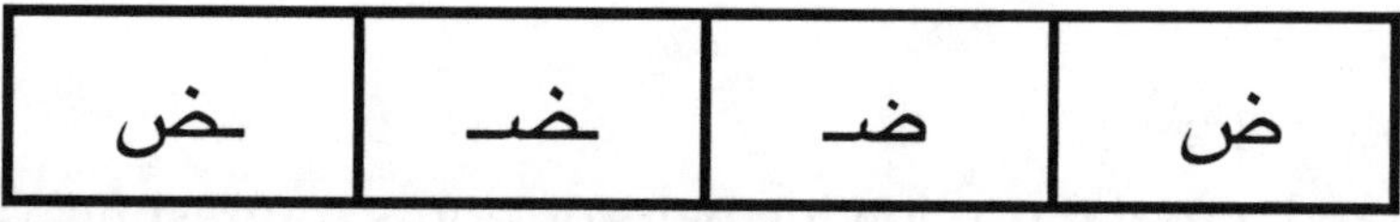

ض is a connector, and is written just like ص except that it takes one dot above. Follow the same steps you did for ص . Practice writing the independent form:

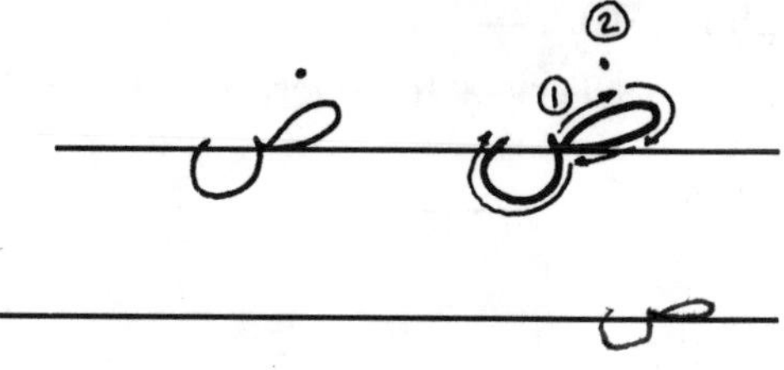

Practice initial ضـ by copying the name of the letter, ضاد :

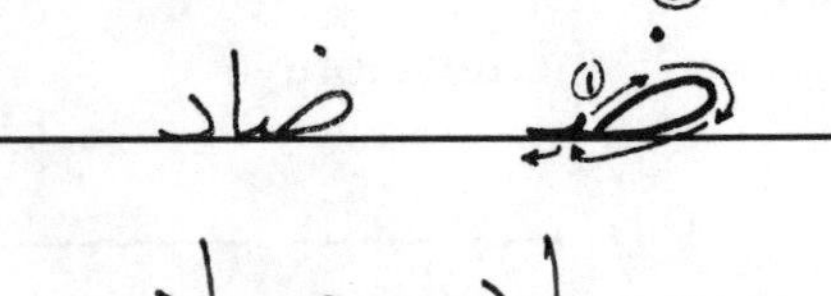

Now practice medial ـضـ by copying أخْضَر (*green*):

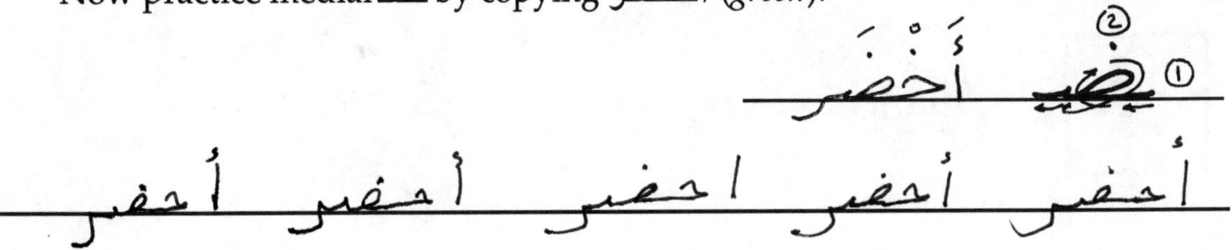

Practice final ـض in بَيْض (*eggs*):

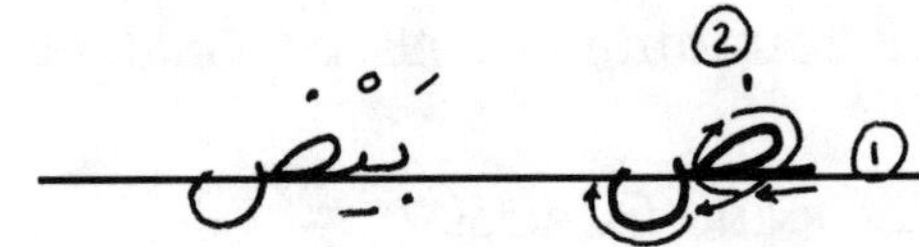

Listening Exercise 8. ⊗⊗

Listen to and repeat the following pairs of words contrasting د and ض :

دال / ضالّ   رِيادة / رِياضة   خَدّ / خَضّ   دَبّ / ضَبّ   دَرْب / ضَرْب

Drill 10. ⊗⊗

Mark **X** for each word in which you hear ض :

1. ______	5. ______	9. ______
2. ______	6. ______	10. ______
3. ______	7. ______	11. ______
4. ______	8. ______	12. ______

Drill 11.

Read the following pairs of words aloud with the tape, paying particular attention to the difference between د and ض :

1. (a) رَدّ (b) رَضّ
2. (a) يَدُرُّ (b) يَضُرُّ
3. (a) تَحَدَّرَت (b) تَحَضَّرَت
4. (a) بيد (b) بيض
5. (a) دَرْبي (b) ضَرْبي
6. (a) دَجَر (b) ضَجَر
7. (a) حَرَّدَت (b) حَرَّضَت
8. (a) دَرَّس (b) ضَرَّس

Drill 12.

You will hear twelve words, each containing either د or ض . Write the letter that corresponds to the sound you hear:

1. _____	5. _____	9. _____
2. _____	6. _____	10. _____
3. _____	7. _____	11. _____
4. _____	8. _____	12. _____

Drill 13.

Listen to the words on tape and write the letter you hear in the blank:

1. ـــباب	4. أ ـــرِب	7. تَـــريس
2. تَحْريـــ	5. ـــحْر	8. أ ـــرار
3. تُبيـــ	6. سرـــي	9. تَـــا ريس

Drill 14.

Connect the letters to form words. Then listen to the words on tape and write in the short vowels you hear.

1.	____________	=	ص + ب + و + ر
2.	____________	=	ش + ب + ا + ب + ي
3.	____________	=	أ + س + ر + ا + ر
4.	____________	=	ت + ص + د + ي + ر
5.	____________	=	ا + س + ت + ي + ر + ا + د
6.	____________	=	ص + و + ا + ر + ي + خ
7.	____________	=	خ + ض + ر + و + ا + ت
8.	____________	=	ش + و + ا + ر + ب
9.	____________	=	ا + ش + ا + ر + ا + ت
10.	____________	=	ص + ب + ا + ح
11.	____________	=	ص + و + ر + ي
12.	____________	=	ص + ر + ا + ص + ي + ر
13.	____________	=	ت + ر + ض + ر + ض + ت
14.	____________	=	ت + خ + ص + ص + ا + ت

Drill 15.

Dictation.

1. ____________
2. ____________
3. ____________
4. ____________
5. ____________
6. ____________
7. ____________
8. ____________
9. ____________
10. ____________

Drill 16.

Read the following words aloud:

أَخْضَر	خَضْراء	أَبْيَض	رَصاص
أَسْوَد	تَسْيير	شَراب	شاي
شَجَر	شِتاء	صُراخ	تَشْريح
سَبْت	صَباح	صَوْت	صَواب
صاحِب	حَواجِز	ضَحايا	إخْراج
أَصْحاب	صَحيح	ضَوْء	تَدْريس
ذُباب	حِساب	حُجَج	زِيارات

Drill 17.

Read the following advertisements, then create five of your own and share with the class.

1.

2.

3.

ايسوزو

4.

إترنتي
ETERNITY

5.

بوبايز
العرض صالح لغاية ٩٢/٩/١٨
بوبايز
الرياض: شارع التخصصي ـ شارع العروبة ـ البديعة ـ شارع العليا ـ المعذر
خميس مشيط: الطريق العسكري ـ الدمام: شارع ابن خلدون

6.

دودج داينستي

7.

دودج سپيريت

من جريدة الشرق الاوسط ، ١٩٩٢

Draw your advertisements here:

1.

2.

3.

4.

5.

CULTURE الثقافة 

VIDEO

Watch Scene 8 with your teacher.

FORMS OF ADDRESS

You have learned to use *HaDritak* (حَضرتَك) and *HaDritik* (حَضرتِك) for polite *you*. In addition, various titles are often used to address people politely. Some of the titles commonly used in Arabic are:

دُكتور / دُكتورة ***duktuur / duktuura*** (Dr.), used to address or refer to medical and academic professionals (whether or not they have a Ph.D.).

أُستاذ / أُستاذة[1] ***ustaadh / ustaadha*** (literally, *teacher, professor*), used to address or refer to an educated person, white-collar employee, schoolteacher, etc.

سَيِّد ***sayyid (Mr.)***, used in formal situations and correspondence to refer to or introduce people who have no professional title.

سَيِّدة ***sayyida (Mrs.)***, and مَدام ***madaam,*** used to address or refer to older and/or married women.

آنِسة ***aanisa (Miss)***, used to address or refer to a young, unmarried woman.

These titles are followed by the person's first or full name (and not by the last name alone). When addressing someone directly, these titles are preceded by *yaa* (يا) (no English equivalent):

yaa duktuur / yaa duktuura	يا دكتور / يا دكتورة
yaa ustaadh Amin	يا استاذ أمين
yaa ustaadha Zeinab	يا استاذة زَيْنَب
yaa aanisa Samia	يا آنسة سامية

[1]Note that these two titles have two common pronunciations: (1) as written above, in formal Arabic, and (2) *ustaaz / ustaaza* in spoken Arabic, as you have heard on the video.

Gender

In the video scenes, you have heard people address and refer to men and women differently: a male professor is addressed or referred to as *duktuur* and a female as *duktuura.* In Arabic, all nouns are either masculine or feminine. That means there is no word for *it* in Arabic, so you must use *he* or *she* depending on what you are talking about. Start practicing this now by thinking of the nouns you learn as *huwa* (he) or *hiya* (she).

Within the category of people, masculine nouns refer to males. To refer to females, these masculine nouns take a feminine ending pronounced *a.* For example, masculine *ustaadh* becomes feminine *ustaadha.* Within the category of inanimate beings or things, each noun has its own gender, which does not change. Masculine words usually end in a consonant, and feminine nouns almost always end in the feminine *a.* There are a few exceptions whose gender must be memorized, but in most cases, you can tell by hearing or reading a word what its gender is.

Drill 18.

Listen to the words on tape. Mark **F** if you hear the feminine *a* and **M** for masculine if you do not:

1. ______
2. ______
3. ______
4. ______
5. ______
6. ______
7. ______
8. ______

الوحدة الخامسة
UNIT FIVE

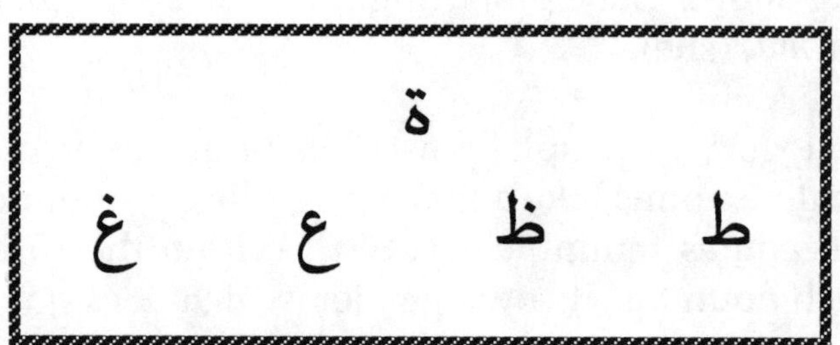

In this unit you will learn the feminine ending ة and the next four consonants in the alphabet.

ة "taa marbuuTa"

This symbol is not considered a part of the Arabic alphabet, because its function is primarily grammatical. It can only occur at the end of a word. This letter is called *taa marbuuTa*, meaning *the tied* ت , and it almost always indicates feminine gender (the rare exceptions to this rule will be noted as they arise). As its name and form indicate, ة is related to the letter ت , and sometimes it is pronounced as ت (you will learn this rule later). At other times it is not pronounced as ت , but **the fatHa vowel that always precedes ة is always pronounced.** In spoken Arabic, a fatHa at the end of a word will almost always indicate ة .

LISTENING EXERCISE 1.

Listen to the following on tape and repeat:

أُستاذة　　　وَردة　　　زَوجة　　　شَجَرة　　　صورة

Remember: when you hear a noun that ends with a fatHa sound, you can usually assume that it is feminine, and spelled with a ة .

Drill 1.

Mark X for each word you hear that ends in ة:

1. ______ 4. ______ 7. ______

2. ______ 5. ______ 8. ______

3. ______ 6. ______ 9. ______

Writing

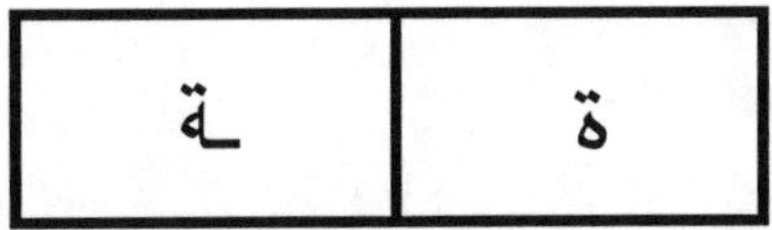

Since ة only occurs in word-final position, it has only two shapes: one that follows connecting letters and one that follows nonconnectors. In print, the two dots appear separately, as you can see, but in handwriting, they are usually drawn together as a short horizontal bar (just like the dots of ت and ي). To write ة after a nonconnecting letter, start above the line at the top of the letter and draw the loop down to your right and back up. Copy the example:

____

____

To write ة connected to a previous letter, start at the connecting segment, draw the right side of the loop up into a point, then swing back down to your left to close the loop. The shape of this loop is usually lopsided and not as round as when ة is written alone, and individual handwriting styles vary. Copy the example:

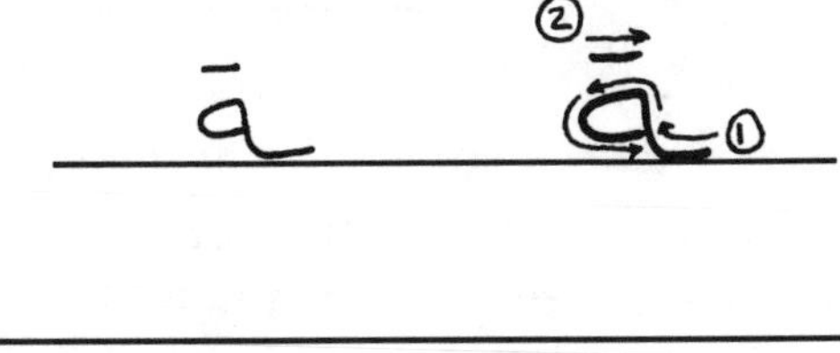

____

____

Now copy and sound out the following words containing ة :

أستاذة　　دِراسة　　سَيِّدة　　جَريدة　　زَوجة　　خارِجيّة

ط "Taa"

This letter represents the emphatic counterpart of ت . To pronounce it, put the tip of your tongue up against the bony ridge behind your teeth on the roof of your mouth, the same position used for ض , and drop your tongue low in your mouth. Try to say *t* holding this position—the result will be ط . The difference in pronunciation between ض and د is the same as the difference between ط and ت . **Remember:** ط is an emphatic sound that deepens the quality of surrounding vowels.

Listening Exercise 2.

Listen to these words containing ط and repeat:

طَبيب　　طالِب　　رُطوبة　　بَطّيخ　　ضابِط　　شُباط

Writing

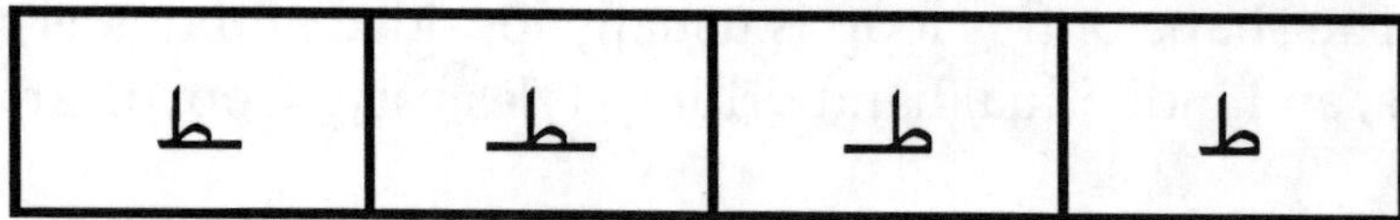

ط is a connector, and is written in two separate steps. The loop that forms the body is written in one motion, connected to the rest of the word, and the vertical line is written afterwards, much like crossing the *t* in English. To write ط independently, start on the line and make the loop first. It should be large and oblong, as in the examples below. The last step in writing ط is the downstroke. After forming the loop, pick up your pen and draw this stroke as you do the alif, from the top down. It does not need to be exactly at the end of the loop.

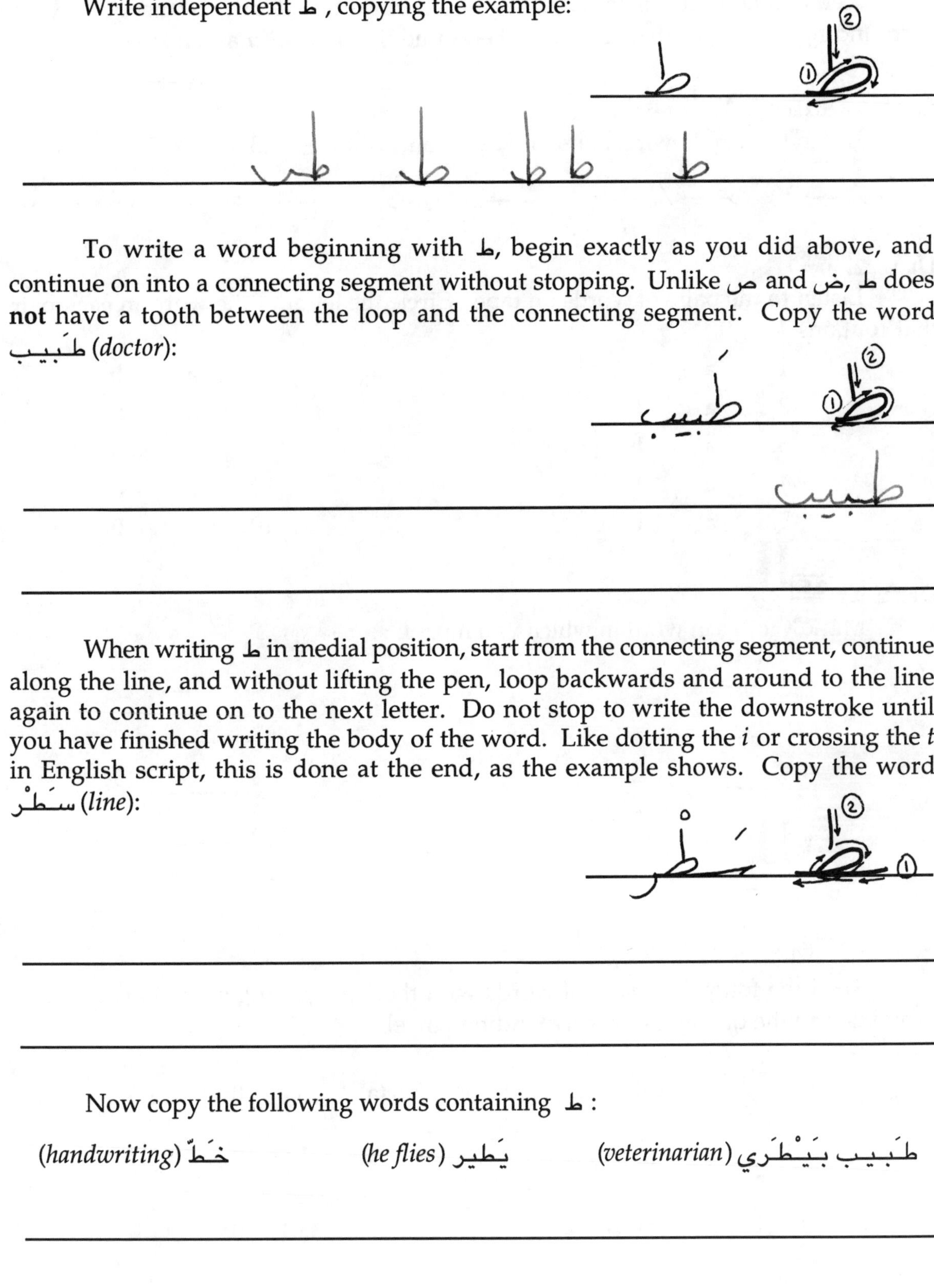

Write independent ط , copying the example:

To write a word beginning with ط, begin exactly as you did above, and continue on into a connecting segment without stopping. Unlike ص and ض, ط does **not** have a tooth between the loop and the connecting segment. Copy the word طَبيب (*doctor*):

When writing ط in medial position, start from the connecting segment, continue along the line, and without lifting the pen, loop backwards and around to the line again to continue on to the next letter. Do not stop to write the downstroke until you have finished writing the body of the word. Like dotting the *i* or crossing the *t* in English script, this is done at the end, as the example shows. Copy the word سَطْر (*line*):

Now copy the following words containing ط :

(*handwriting*) خَطّ (*he flies*) يَطير (*veterinarian*) طَبيب بَيْطَري

Remember that, since ط is an emphatic letter, it affects the quality of surrounding vowels, so that alif and fatHa sound like *a* in *father* and *u* in *but*.

Listening Exercise 3.

Listen to the following pairs of words contrasting ت and ط :

تاب / طاب   شَتّ / شَطّ   رَتَّبَ / رَطَّبَ   سَتْر / سَطْر   حَتّ / حَطّ

Drill 2.

Listen to the pairs of words on tape. Circle the letter of the word in each pair that contains ط :

1.	a	b	6.	a	b
2.	a	b	7.	a	b
3.	a	b	8.	a	b
4.	a	b	9.	a	b
5.	a	b	10.	a	b

Drill 3.

Mark X for each word in which you hear ط :

1. ____	6. ____
2. ____	7. ____
3. ____	8. ____
4. ____	9. ____
5. ____	10. ____

Drill 4.

Read the following pairs of words with the tape, paying special attention to ت and ط and the quality of the surrounding vowels:

1. (a) أَوْتار (b) أَوْطار
2. (a) رَتيب (b) رَطيب
3. (a) وَتْوات (b) وَطْواط
4. (a) بَتّ (b) بَطّ
5. (a) وَتَّر (b) وَطَّد
6. (a) أَتْرَح (b) أَطْرَح
7. (a) تَيّار (b) طَيّار
8. (a) توب (b) طوب

Drill 5.

Listen to the words on tape and write the letter you hear in the blank:

1. حَـــــب	4. خَـــــ	7. دُسـ ـــــور
2. رابـــــة	5. ـــــبْشورة	8. شَـــــِاء
3. ـــــزْخَر	6. سُـــــور	9. بُحـ ـــــ

Drill 6.

Dictation.

1. ______________

2. ______________

3. ______________

4. ______________

5. ______________

6. ______________

"DHaa"

This letter represents the emphatic counterpart of ذ . Place your tongue in the same position as you did for ط, and try to say ذ . The tip of your tongue should be between your teeth, but the rest of your tongue should remain in the same position as for ط, low in the mouth. **Remember:** ظ is an emphatic sound that deepens the quality of surrounding vowels.

Listening Exercise 4.

Listen to the words on tape and repeat, paying attention to the vowel quality around ظ :

أبو ظَبي   ظالِم   شَظِيّة   حَظّ   ظُهور

WRITING

ظ	ـظ	ـظـ	ظـ

ظ is a connector, and is written like ط in all positions, with the addition of one dot above the body of the letter. Follow the arrows to write independent ظ :

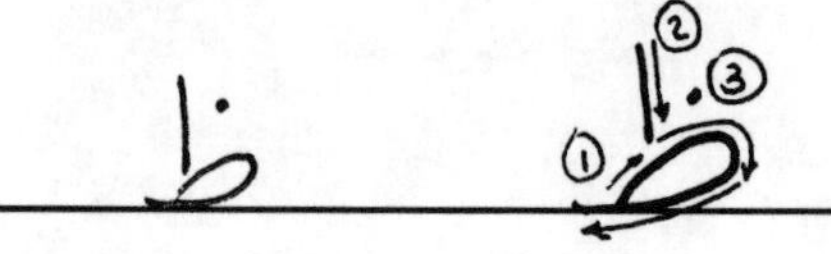

When writing initial and medial ظ , **do not stop** to "cross" and dot ظ until you have finished writing the skeleton of the word. Copy the name of the Arab Emirate, أبو ظَبي , as shown:

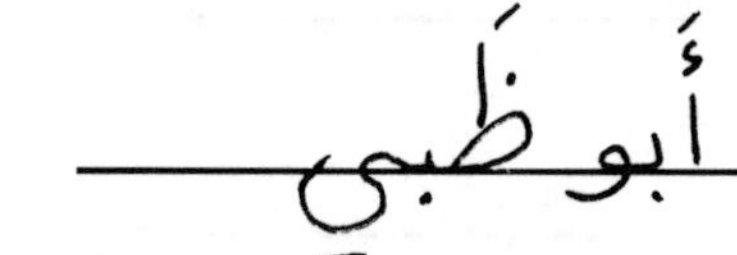

Copy and sound out the following words containing ظ :

(*luck*) حَظّ (*ice cream*) بوظة (*gazelle*) ظَبي

LISTENING EXERCISE 5.

Listen to the contrast between ذ and ظ in the following pairs of words:

ذال / ظاء ذَنْب / ظَنّ حَذَر / حَظَر ذَلّ / ظَلّ نَذَر / نَظَر

Drill 7.

Listen to the pairs of words on tape. For each pair, circle the letter of the word that contains ظ :

1.	a	b	6.	a	b
2.	a	b	7.	a	b
3.	a	b	8.	a	b
4.	a	b	9.	a	b
5.	a	b	10.	a	b

Listening Exercise 6.

Recognition of ث, ذ, ض, and ظ. Listen to the following words on tape to review these sounds:

1.	(a) ظَبْي	(b) ضابِط	(c) ذابَت	(d) ثابِت
2.	(a) حَظَر	(b) حَضَر	(c) حَذَر	(d) حَثّ
3.	(a) بَظّ	(b) بَضّ	(c) بَذّ	(d) بَثّ

Drill 8.

You will hear ten words. For each, circle the sound you hear:

1.	ظ	ض	ذ	ث	6.	ظ	ض	ذ	ث
2.	ظ	ض	ذ	ث	7.	ظ	ض	ذ	ث
3.	ظ	ض	ذ	ث	8.	ظ	ض	ذ	ث
4.	ظ	ض	ذ	ث	9.	ظ	ض	ذ	ث
5.	ظ	ض	ذ	ث	10.	ظ	ض	ذ	ث

Drill 9.

Read the following aloud with the tape, paying attention to ث , ذ , and ظ :

1.	(a) ثَبَت	(b) ذُباب	(c) ظَبْيَة
2.	(a) حُثّي	(b) حوذي	(c) حَظّي
3.	(a) يَحُثُّ	(b) يَحذو	(c) يَحظو
4.	(a) أثَّر	(b) حَذَّر	(c) حَظَّر

Drill 10.

Listen to the words on tape and write the letter you hear in the blank:

1. ـــبي
2. تَحْـــير
3. حَـــ
4. أ ـــواب
5. أ ـــرِياء
6. ـــبْت
7. حِـــاء
8. إِ ـــبات
9. ـــبْط
10. جَـــوة
11. حَـــيّة
12. بُـــور

Drill 11.

Dictation.

1. ______________
2. ______________
3. ______________
4. ______________
5. ______________
6. ______________
7. ______________
8. ______________

Drill 12.

Read the following pairs of nouns aloud:

ضَرورة ضَرورات	حاجّ حُجّاج	دار دور
أُستاذة أُستاذات	حِزْب أحْزاب	حارة حارات
طَبيب أطِبّاء	طَبيبة طَبيبات	صورة صُوَر
سَيّارة سَيّارات	أُسْتاذ أساتِذة	طَيْر طُيور
شَيْخ شُيوخ	يَخْت يُخوت	جُثّة جُثَث
ضابِط ضُبّاط	واجِب واجِبات	ظَبْية ظِباء

What can you guess about the relationship between each pair of nouns?

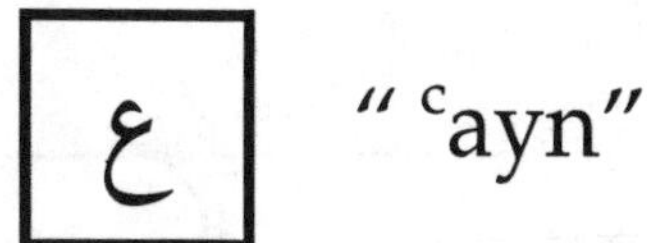

" ᶜayn"

We now come to one of the most distinctive sounds in Arabic: ع . When pronounced correctly, ع has its own unique beauty and can be a very expressive sound. The degree to which ع is emphasized differs slightly from one dialect area to another; in the Gulf and some areas of North Africa, it is pronounced with a greater constricting of the muscles and has a more powerful sound. It is not difficult to pronounce, but you need to exercise your throat muscles, the same ones that you use to pronounce ح . You should still be doing the exercises you learned above for ح , in which you constrict your throat muscles as if you were blocking off the air passage from the inside. You can feel this by putting your hand on your throat. Say ح , and feel the muscles contract. Now pronounce the same sound and voice it, that is, instead of a breathy sound, make a deep, throaty sound. Keep your hand on your throat so that you can feel your muscles contracting. Also, if you bend your head down so that your chin rests on your chest, you will be able to feel and hear what you are doing more easily.

Listening Exercise 7.

Listen to ع in the following words and repeat several times:

عَرَبي   عَيْب   عاد   يَعود   ساعة   رَعْي   دَع

It is helpful to put your hand to your throat or bend your head down and put your chin on your chest so that you can feel the muscles contract every time you say ع for a while, until you can say it easily. ع is a very important sound in Arabic, and you must learn to say it properly in order to be understood. The more you practice now, the sooner ع will become natural for you.

Writing

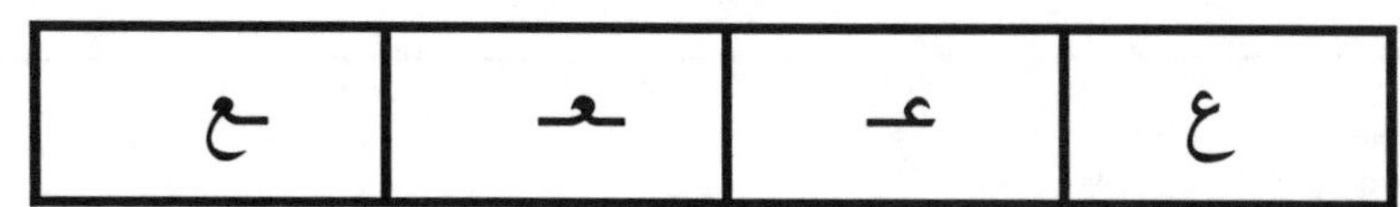

ع is a connecting letter whose shape varies somewhat depending on its position. In independent and initial positions, the common element is a c-shape that rests on the line. As an independent letter, it takes a tail, when connected to a following letter, it leads into a connecting segment as shown. Practice writing and pronouncing independent ع as shown:

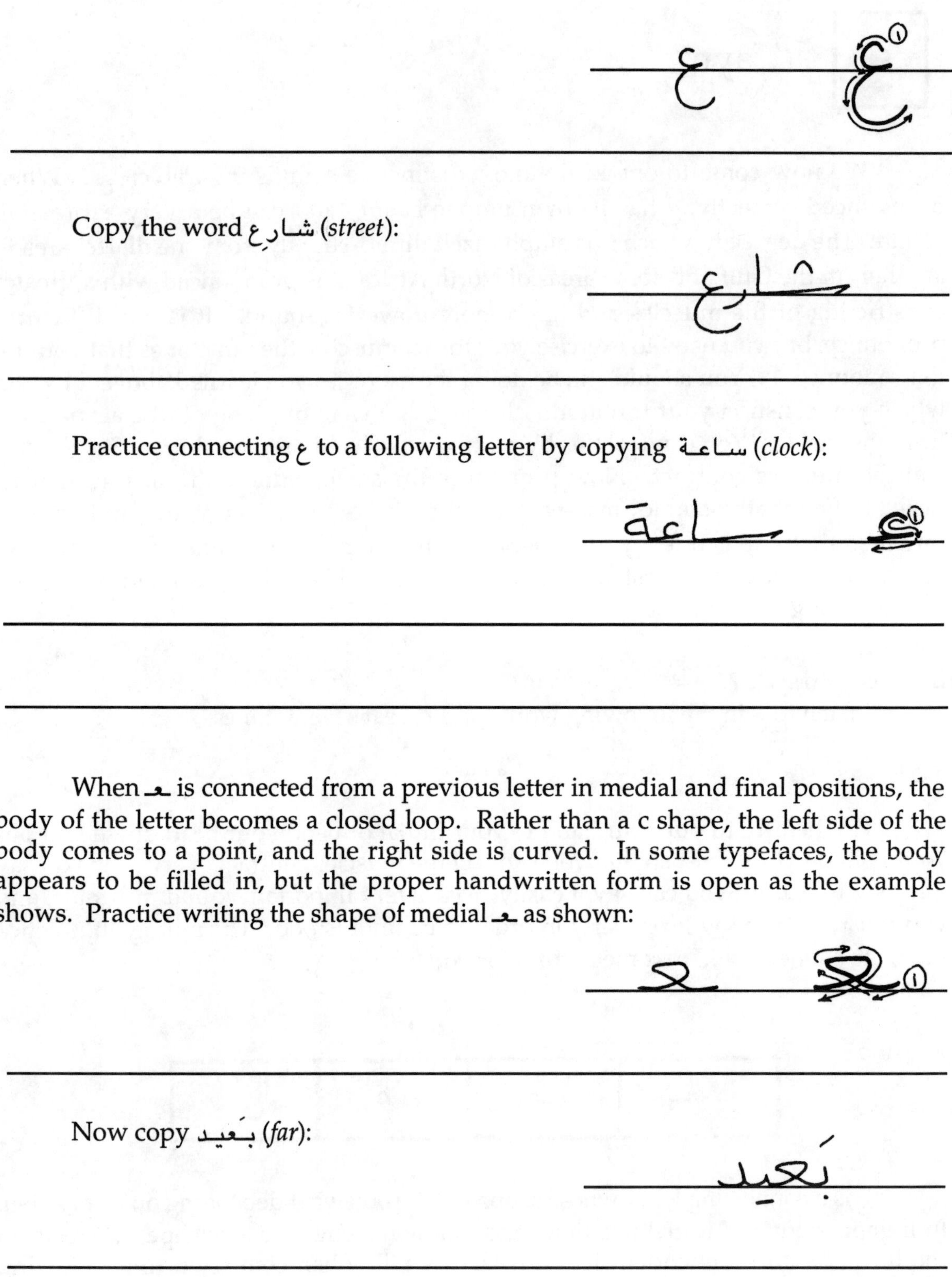

Copy the word شارِع (*street*):

Practice connecting ع to a following letter by copying ساعة (*clock*):

When ـعـ is connected from a previous letter in medial and final positions, the body of the letter becomes a closed loop. Rather than a c shape, the left side of the body comes to a point, and the right side is curved. In some typefaces, the body appears to be filled in, but the proper handwritten form is open as the example shows. Practice writing the shape of medial ـعـ as shown:

Now copy بَعيد (*far*):

In final position, ـع reassumes its tail. Practice by copying أَربَع (*four*):

أَربَع

Listening Exercise 8.

Listen to the following pairs of words and repeat, paying attention to the pronunciation of ء and ع . Remember that ء is a sound you produce naturally, without effort. Say *uh-oh* before pronouncing ء , and put your hand on your throat when pronouncing ع .

وأَدَ / وَعَدَ   تَأَثَّرَ / تَعَثَّرَ   أسير / عَسير   أبَد / عَبَد   أطَّر / عَطَّر

Drill 13.

Read the following words aloud with the tape, paying special attention to the difference between ع and ء :

1.	(a) أَيَّدَت	(b) عَيَّدَت		6.	(a) أزيز	(b) عَزيز
2.	(a) إبْرة	(b) عِبْرة		7.	(a) جَأْجَأَ	(b) جَعْجَع
3.	(a) تَعَطَّرَ	(b) تَأَطَّرَ		8.	(a) شاءَ	(b) شاعَ
4.	(a) رَأْي	(b) رَعْي		9.	(a) صَدَأَ	(b) صَدَعَ
5.	(a) جاءَت	(b) جاعَت		10.	(a) أَجْزَأَت	(b) أَجْزَعَت

Drill 14.

Circle the sound you hear:

1.	ع ء		4.	ع ء		7.	ع ء
2.	ع ء		5.	ع ء		8.	ع ء
3.	ع ء		6.	ع ء		9.	ع ء

Drill 15.

Listen to the words on tape and write the letter you hear in the blank:

1. ـــطْر	4. ـــحِبّ	7. صَـــب
2. رَـــد	5. ـــودي	8. ثَـــري
3. شارِ ـــ	6. دَـــوات	9. تَســـير

Drill 16.

Dictation.

1. ______________ 5. ______________

2. ______________ 6. ______________

3. ______________ 7. ______________

4. ______________ 8. ______________

Copy and sound out the following names:

 سُعاد سَعدِيّة دَعْد عَطِيّات عَبير

____

____

♂ سَعيد أَسعَد عُبَيْد ساطِع عَبّاس

____

____

غ	"ghayn"

This letter is pronounced like a voiced خ. Think of the correspondence between the sounds *k* (*kite*) and *g* (*game*): *k* is unvoiced and *g* is voiced. Pronounce *k* and *g* several times, paying attention to how your voice changes when you say *g*. Now say خ several times, then voice it. Alternatively, you may think of غ as similar to the sound you make when gargling. Gargle for a minute and pay attention to the muscles that you use. غ is pronounced using these same muscles in similar fashion.

LISTENING EXERCISE 9.

Listen to غ in these words and repeat:

غَريب   بَغداد   صَغير   طاغي   تَبغ   غُربة

WRITING

ـغ	ـغـ	غـ	غ

غ is a connector, and has the same shapes as ع , except that it takes a single dot above. First, practice independent غ as shown, pronouncing it aloud as you write:

غ غ

Now write صاغ (*piaster*, Egyptian coin roughly equivalent to a penny):

صاغ

Initial غـ connects to a following letter as shown. Practice writing and pronouncing the word غَـبـي (*stupid*). Do not stop to dot until you have finished writing the entire word:

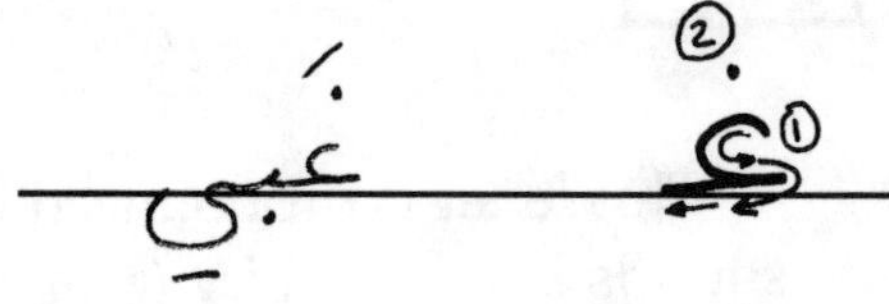

Medial ـغـ is written just like medial ـعـ. Copy and pronounce بَـغـداد :

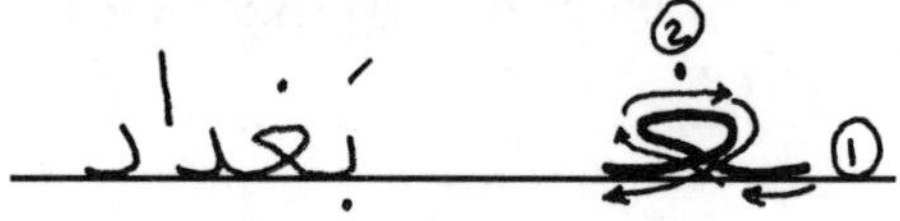

Final ـغ assumes the long tail. Practice by copying and saying تَـبـغ (*tobacco*):

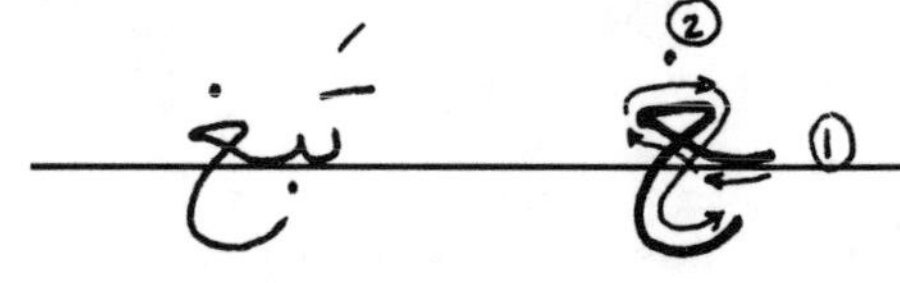

Listening Exercise 10.

Compare the following pairs of words on tape, paying particular attention to the difference between غ and خ :

يَـغيـب / يَـخيـب   غَـضّ / خَـضّ   يُـغَـرِّب/يُـخَـرِّب   تَـغُـصّ /تَـخُـصّ

Drill 17. 🖭

You will hear nine words. Circle the letter corresponding to the sound you hear:

1.	خ	غ	4.	خ	غ	7.	خ	غ
2.	خ	غ	5.	خ	غ	8.	خ	غ
3.	خ	غ	6.	خ	غ	9.	خ	غ

Drill 18. 🖭

Read the following pairs of words aloud with the tape, paying close attention to غ and خ :

1. **(a)** تَخريب **(b)** تَغريب
2. **(a)** يَشخُر **(b)** يَشغُر
3. **(a)** خَيْري **(b)** غَيْري
4. **(a)** بَخْت **(b)** بَغْت
5. **(a)** خَيْبة **(b)** غَيْبة
6. **(a)** رَخْوة **(b)** رَغْوة
7. **(a)** خَرير **(b)** غَرير
8. **(a)** تَخُطّ **(b)** تَغُطّ
9. **(a)** خَبَّط **(b)** غَبَّط
10. **(a)** خَضير **(b)** غَضير

Drill 19. 🖭

Listen to the words on tape and write the letter you hear in the blank:

1. صَـــير
2. تَـــيُّر
3. ـــزّة
4. شَـــب
5. ـــياطة
6. طا ـــية
7. سُـــرية
8. تَـــرُجي
9. ضَـــط

Drill 20. 🖭

Read the following words aloud:

عُصور طِراز صُراخ عَصَبيّة طاسات عَشاء

تَبْشير جُبّة خَطيبَتي أبو ظَبي غاضِبة طازة

يُدَثِّر صُروح أعْداء طَبْشورة تَسريحة ذَوْد

غَداء إشْعارات بُذور تَصْدير اِرْتِباطات شُعَراء

DRILL 21.

Connect the letters to form words and sound them out.

1. ________________ = صَ + ر + ا + ح + ة
2. ________________ = تَ + غَ + يُّ + ر + ا + ت
3. ________________ = بَ + ع + ي + د
4. ________________ = شَ + خْ + صِ + يّ + ة
5. ________________ = تَ + صْ + غ + ي + ر
6. ________________ = طُ + ر + و + د + ي
7. ________________ = اِ + عْ + تِ + ر + ا + ض
8. ________________ = غَ + رْ + بِ + يّ + ة
9. ________________ = أَ + طِ + بّ + ا + ء
10. ________________ = شَ + ظ + ا + ي + ا
11. ________________ = ضَ + و + ا + ح + ي
12. ________________ = اِ + سْ + تَ + غ + رَ + بَ
13. ________________ = تَ + خَ + صُّ + ص
14. ________________ = رُ + سْ + غ

Drill 22.

You will hear ten words. Circle the word you hear in each row:

1.	غَرب	خَرَّب	جَرَب	حَرْب
2.	ضَرَس	دَرَّس	دَرَز	دَرَس
3.	أسبَح	اِطْبَع	إصْبَع	أصبَح
4.	ذاع	صاع	ضاع	شاع
5.	صَغير	سَرير	صَرير	شِرّير
6.	حُثّ	جِصّ	حِصّ	حِسّ
7.	فَرّخ	فَرْخ	فَزَع	فَرْع
8.	حَذَر	حَصَر	حَظَر	حَضَر
9.	ضَبي	سَبي	صَبي	ظَبي
10.	غَبَّر	عِبَر	عَبَّر	أَبَرّ

Drill 23.

Dictation.

1. ____________	6. ____________
2. ____________	7. ____________
3. ____________	8. ____________
4. ____________	9. ____________
5. ____________	10. ____________

Read and learn these words:

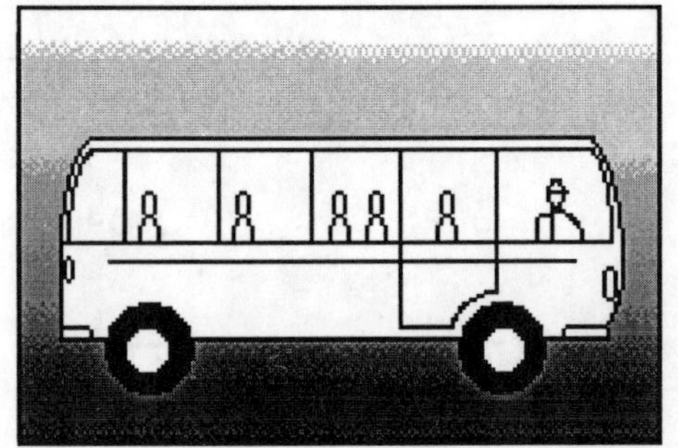

أوتوبيس

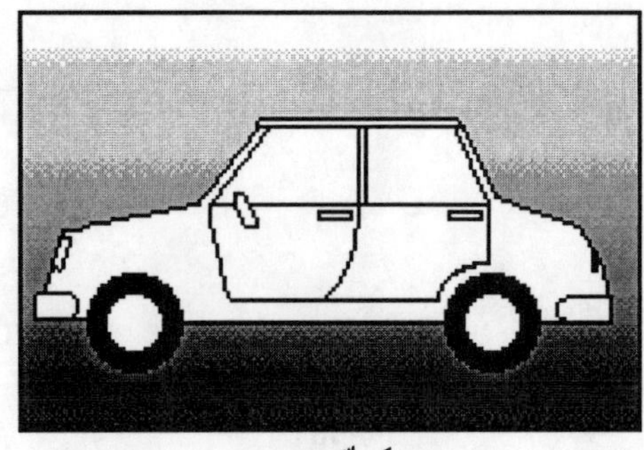

سَيّارة

شارِع

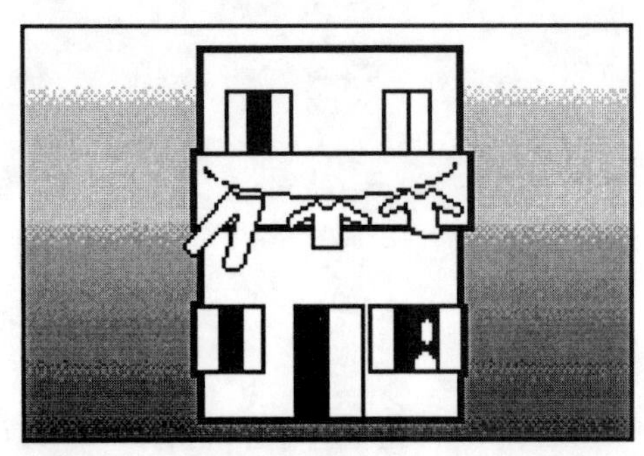

بَيْت

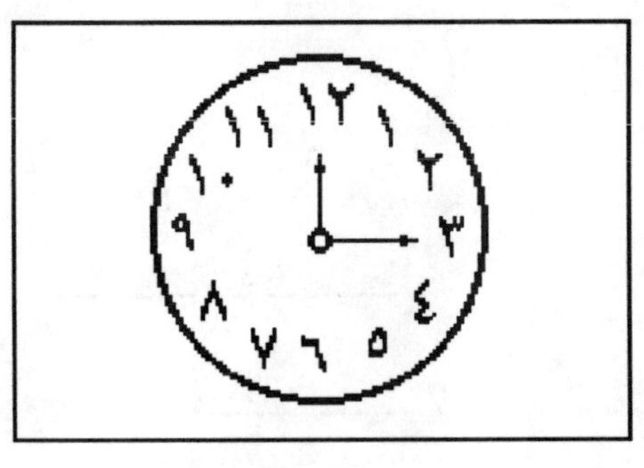

ساعة

أُستاذ

wide, spacious	واسِع / ـة	lesson	دَرْس
small	صَغير / ة	Arab (person), Arabic	عَرَبي / ـة
hard, difficult	صَعْب / ـة	new	جَديد / ة

Drill 24.

Read each of the following phrases aloud, then write its meaning in the blank.

1. *an Arab teacher (professor)* ____ أُستاذ عَرَبي
2. ________________ أُستاذة عَرَبِيّة
3. ________________ دَرْس صَعْب
4. ________________ شارِع صَغير
5. ________________ سَيّارة جَديدة
6. ________________ سيّارة صغيرة
7. ________________ أوتوبيس جديد
8. ________________ أوتوبيس صغير
9. ________________ أستاذ صعب
10. ________________ بَيْت جديد
11. ________________ بَيت واسِع
12. ________________ بيت صغير
13. ________________ شارع واسع
14. ________________ ساعة صغيرة
15. ________________ درس جديد
16. ________________ أستاذة جديدة
17. ________________ بيت عربي
18. ________________ ساعة جديدة

CULTURE الثقافة 

VIDEO

Watch Scenes 9, 10, and 11 with your teacher.

TAKING LEAVE

Just as greeting people when you first see them is essential to courteous behavior, taking leave is also expected. Whether sitting at a meal or just standing around chatting, you must excuse yourself before leaving. People usually say:

ᶜan iznak / ᶜan iznik[1] عَن إذنَك / عَن إذنِك

which means *with your permission*, and the usual response is:

itfaDDal / itfaDDali اِتفَضَّل / اِتفَضَّلي

which means *please, go ahead.* You have also heard *itfaDDal/i* used to mean *please, come in / sit down*, and it can also mean *please, help yourself* (for example, to food).

---

[1]Remember that in Egypt, ذ is often pronounced z.

الوحدة السادسة

UNIT SIX

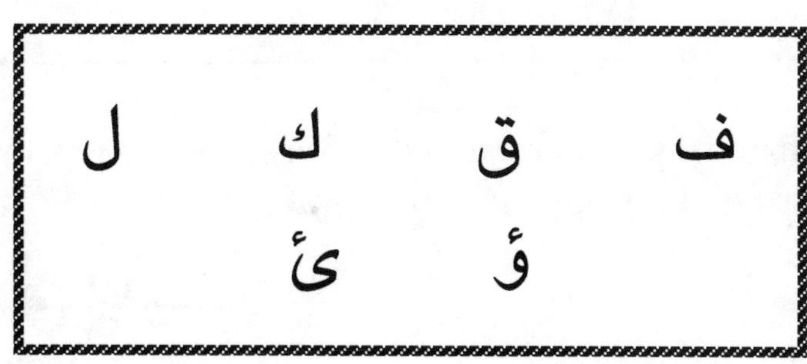

In this unit you will learn four new consonants and two new seats for hamza.

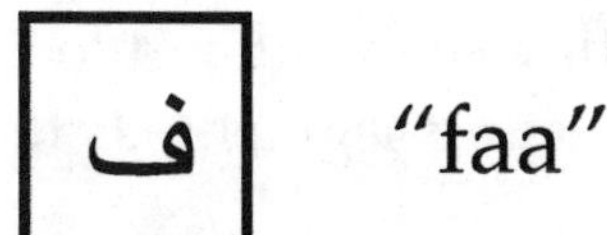

ف "faa"

This letter is pronounced like English *f* as in *feather*.

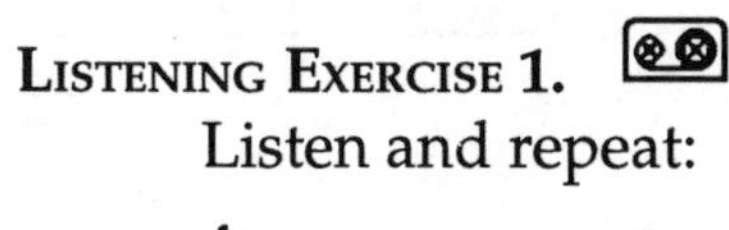

Listening Exercise 1.

Listen and repeat:

فَرَح   فَريد   دَفْتَر   سَفير   عَفاف   صُفوف

Writing

ـف	ـفـ	فـ	ف

ف is a connecting letter with a relatively stable shape. Its independent and final forms have a tail that is unusual in that it remains on the line rather than dipping below. To write independent ف , begin above the line and draw a small flat loop around to your left, up, and down around. Keep the loop of ف small and just above the line, resting on a short "neck." Continue along the line into a small hook to finish the tail as shown in the example below.

Practice writing independent ف :

ف

To write فـ in initial position, begin the same way and finish with a connecting segment into the next letter. Copy the name فَريد :

فَريد

The loop of medial ـفـ is small and oval (for example, it is **much** smaller than that of ـطـ , and has a different shape). Start from the connecting segment and loop up to your left and back around to the line and into the connecting segment, as the example shows:

ـفـ

Now write سَفير (*ambassador*):

سَفير

Final ـف combines the shape of the medial position with the tail of the independent ف . Copy صَفّ (*class*):

صَفّ

Copy and sound out the following names:

♀ عَفاف فَرَح فَريدة وَفاء صَفاء صَفيّة

♂ فَريد عَفيف فَتْحي فايِز فَوْزي رِفْعَت

Drill 1.
Dictation.

1. ____________ 4. ____________

2. ____________ 5. ____________

3. ____________ 6. ____________

ق "qaaf"

This letter represents a new sound, the emphatic counterpart to *k*. Like the other emphatic sounds, it is pronounced with the tongue low in the mouth. It differs from them in that it is pronounced farther back in the throat, at the very back of the tongue. Take a minute to become more familiar with your throat muscles. Open your mouth and say *aah,* as if you were at the doctor's. Your tongue should be flat in your mouth. Without raising your tongue, pull it back so that the base of your tongue closes off air by pulling back against the throat. At this point, you should not be able to breathe through your mouth, although it is wide open. Practice doing this first without making a sound. After performing this exercise several times, make a sound by releasing the air forcefully. The result will be the sound ق .

Listening Exercise 2.

Listen to ق in the following words and repeat:

قاف   قارِب   دَقيقة   شَفيق   بَرقوق   فِراق

Drill 2.

Mark X for each word in which you hear ق :

1. ________ 4. ________ 7. ________

2. ________ 5. ________ 8. ________

3. ________ 6. ________ 9. ________

Writing

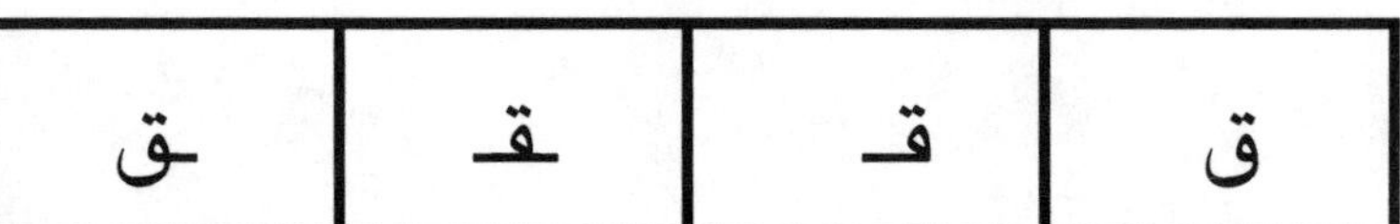

ق is a connector, and its shape is similar to that of ف in all positions, except that ق takes two dots above and a deep tail that drops well below the line like that of س and ص . The two dots above ق are usually run together in handwriting (like those of ت). To write independent ق , make the same loop you made for ف , then drop below the line to draw the tail and **make sure to bring the tail all the way back up to the line.** Copy the example:

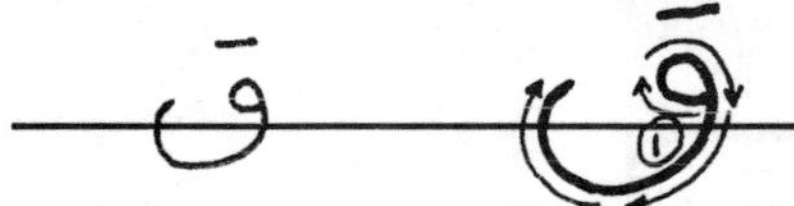

Initial ـقـ is written just like initial ـفـ , but with two dots run together. Copy the example:

Practice by writing قَريب (*near*). Do not stop to dot until you have finished writing the word:

Medial ـقـ has the same shape and size as medial ـفـ, and is connected in the same way. Practice by writing دَقيقة (*minute*):

Unlike final ـف, final ـق takes a tail that drops well below the line, just like that of س. Make sure to bring it all the way back up to the line:

Practice final ـق by writing بَرقوق (*plum*):

Drill 3.

Dictation.

1. __________

2. __________

3. __________

4. __________

5. __________

6. __________

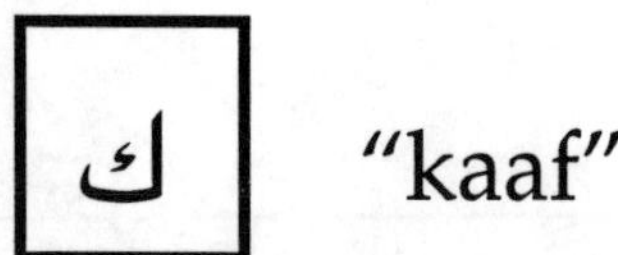

"kaaf"

This letter corresponds to English k as in *likewise*.[1]

Listening Exercise 3.

Listen to ك in the following words and repeat:

رَكيك   شُكوك   أكيد   حِكاية   دُكتور   كِتاب

Writing

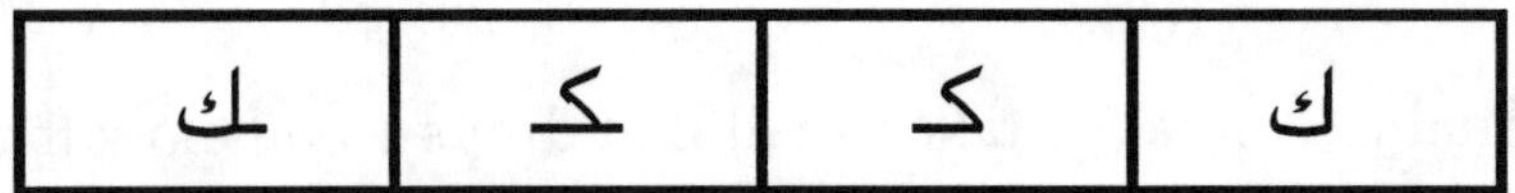

ك is a connecting letter that has two distinct shapes, one in independent and final positions, and one in initial and medial positions. To write independent ك , start above the line at the top of the letter, draw straight down to the line, then curve and follow the line. Make a tiny hook at the end, then pick up your pen and draw a little hamza-like figure inside the angle. The shape of this mark, which may have originated as a miniature ک , may vary slightly in different scripts. Copy the example:

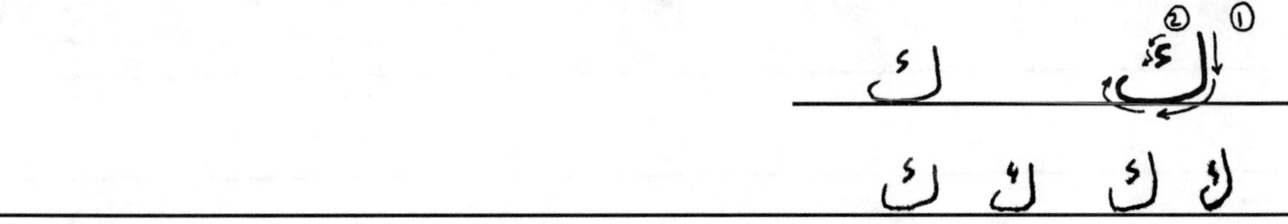

When ک is connected to a following letter, it has a cross bar on the top; however, this is written last, like the vertical bar of ط and ظ . To write initial ک , start as you do the independent form, drawing down to the line, then make a right angle and draw along it into a connecting segment. Note that the body of initial ک is not exactly perpendicular to the line on the paper—it may be slightly slanted or even curved, depending on individual style. After you finish writing the skeleton of the word, go back and "cross" the ک as shown (it does not matter if the bar is not

[1] Note that Arabic ك is never aspirated, that is , it has no "breathy" sound like that of *k* in *kite*.

exactly lined up, but keep it as close as possible). Copy initial ﻛ , following the arrows:

Now practice writing initial ﻛ in كَبير (*big*):

Medial ﻜ is written like initial ﻛ , except that you must start from a connecting segment on the line and draw up, then trace the same line back down. (Again, the body does not have to be exactly perpendicular to the line, and its exact angle may vary somewhat.) Wait until you finish writing the word to draw the cross bar. Copy:

Practice writing medial ﻜ in فِكرة (*idea*):

In certain artistic scripts and fonts, ﻛ takes a slightly different shape. Find ﻛ in each of these words:

دكتور دكتور دكتور اسكندرية اسكندرية اسكندرية

Be prepared to recognize ﻛ when written this way.

Final ـك is similar in shape to independent ك except that it is connected to the previous letter. Start from the connecting segment, draw a line up, roughly perpendicular to the line, then trace it back down, and give it a flat tail along the line (the same tail you draw for ـف). When you have finished writing, give it the little hamza-like mark as in the example:

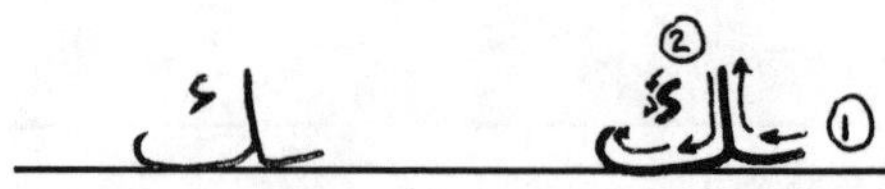

Practice final ـك by writing شيك (*check*):

ك represents a familiar sound that takes no extra effort on your part. Take care to distinguish between it and ق , which is pronounced deep in the throat and which you must **practice**. **Remember:** ق is an emphatic letter that deepens the quality of surrounding vowels, whereas vowels surrounding ك are frontal.

Listening Exercise 4.

Listen to the difference between ك and ق in the following pairs of words and repeat:

قَدَّس / كَدَّس   رَقيق/رَكيك   قابوس/كابوس   باقِر/باكِر   شَقّ /شَكّ

Drill 4.

You will hear twelve words. Circle the sound you hear in each:

1.	ق	ك	5.	ق	ك	9.	ق	ك
2.	ق	ك	6.	ق	ك	10.	ق	ك
3.	ق	ك	7.	ق	ك	11.	ق	ك
4.	ق	ك	8.	ق	ك	12.	ق	ك

Drill 5.

Read these words aloud with the tape, paying special attention to ك and ق and the quality of the surrounding vowels:

1. (a)	كادَ	(b)	قادَ	6. (a)	بَكَرَ	(b)	بَقَرَ
2. (a)	شُكوك	(b)	شُقوق	7. (a)	صَدَّكَ	(b)	صَدَّقَ
3. (a)	كَسْوة	(b)	قَسْوة	8. (a)	اِكتِفاء	(b)	اِقتِفاء
4. (a)	كَدَّر	(b)	قَدَّر	9. (a)	عِراك	(b)	عِراق
5. (a)	حَبَك	(b)	حَبَق	10. (a)	كُروش	(b)	قُروش

Drill 6.

Write the letter that you hear in each blank:

1. ___ريب	4. ضَيِّـ___	7. حَظُّ___
2. بِطا___ة	5. اِستشرا___	8. فِـ___رة
3. صد___ور	6. را___ص	9. سُـ___ر

Drill 7.

Dictation.

1. ____________
2. ____________
3. ____________
4. ____________
5. ____________
6. ____________
7. ____________
8. ____________

Read and copy these names:

♀ رُقَيّة شَريفة كَوثَر شَفيقة فَيروز وَفاء

____

____

♂ شَوكَت طارِق شُكري تَوفيق شَفيق زَكَريّا

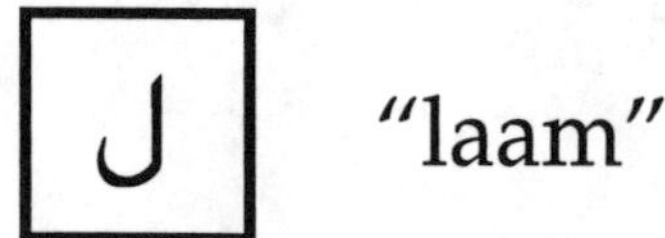

This letter represents the sound of the Spanish or French *l*, that is, a frontal *l* in which the front part of the tongue is against the back of the teeth, and the tongue is high in the mouth. Americans tend to pronounce *l* with the tongue farther back and lower down in the mouth, resulting in a more emphatic sound than Arabic ل . Say the word *terrible* aloud, and pay attention to the position of your tongue when you say *ble*. It is similar to the position your tongue holds when you say ص , ض , and ط. To pronounce Arabic ل , hold the tip of your tongue against the back of your teeth at the roof of your mouth and keep your tongue as high and frontal as you can. Practice this position while imitating the words you hear on tape.

Listening Exercise 5.

Listen to and repeat the following words containing the sound ل , paying particular attention to the **frontal** quality of the surrounding vowels:

ليبيا حَليب عالِية حُلول طَويل صَليب طَلَعَ

As you may have noticed listening to the words طَلَعَ and صَليب in the above exercise, ل can take on an emphatic quality when it occurs near emphatic consonants. To pronounce emphatic ل , keep the front part of your tongue pressed against the back of your teeth, and drop the rest of your tongue low in your mouth. Repeat Listening Exercise 5, paying attention to the pronunciation of ل in its different environments. Only one word in Arabic has a ل emphatic in quality without outside influence, and that is the word for God, *Allaah*. (In some cases, this word is pronounced with a regular ل —you will learn this rule later.) Listening Exercise 6 introduces you to some common expressions that include the word *Allaah*.

Listening Exercise 6.

Listen to these expressions containing the word *Allaah*:

(expresses admiration or delight)	*Allaah!*	الله!
God willing	*in shaa'Allaah*	إن شاءَ الله
(used when praising or admiring)	*maa shaa'Allaah*	ما شاءَ الله!
There is no god but God (said upon hearing bad news)	*laa ilaaha illa Allaah*	لا إله إلاّ الله
May God have mercy on him (=May he rest in peace)	*Allaah yirHamuh*	الله يِرحَمُه
In the name of God (said upon beginning something)	*bismillaah*	بِسْمِ الله

Writing

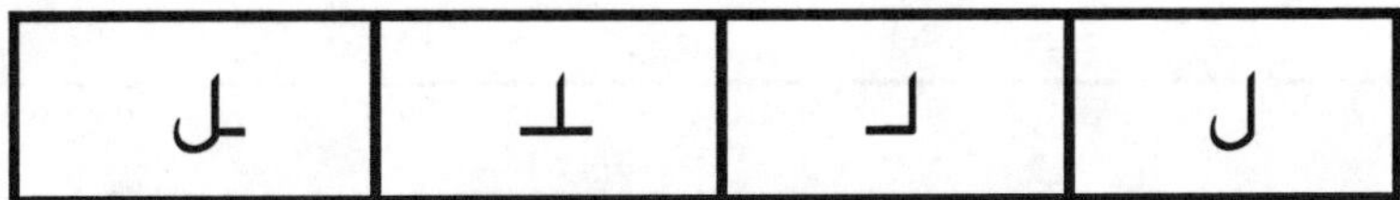

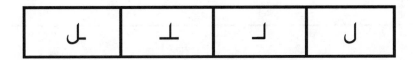

ل is a connecting letter. The shapes of ل are similar to those of ك except that ل has no cross bar and has a narrower and deeper tail that dips below the line in its independent and final positions. Note how similar the shapes of medial ـا (alif) and ـلـ appear: the only difference is that ـلـ connects, while alif does not.

To write independent ل, start at the top and draw straight down, continuing below the line into the tail, which should be approximately the same shape as the tail of س, but a little narrower. **The tail must come all the way back up above the line.** Copy:

ل ل

Initial لـ is begun the same way, down to the line. Rather than drawing the tail, continue into the connecting segment along the line:

لـ لـ

Practice writing initial لـ in ليبيا :

To write medial ـلـ , start from the connecting segment, draw up and then trace back down to the line into the next connecting segment as shown:

Practice ـلـ by copying بَلَد (*country*):

Follow the same procedure to write final ـل , but finish with the tail:

Practice by writing طَويل (*long*):

لا "laam alif"

The distinct shape of the combination of ا+ل (laam followed by alif) is not part of the Arabic alphabet, but must be used to join these letters wherever they occur in this order in the same word. This shape varies slightly in print and handwriting styles. The form you see in the box above is the one you will see in print. Some people write it this way by hand as well, in one stroke (your teacher can show you how). In most handwriting styles, the laam and alif retain the angles you see above, but the two letters are written in two separate strokes. To produce لا in this handwritten form, start as you would connected ـل , but instead of drawing the body straight down, draw it slanting down to the left. When you reach the line, pick up your pen and make a slanted alif stroke into the corner of ـل as the example shows. Write the word لا , which means *no*:

لا

Remember that the alif does not connect to a following letter, therefore, لا **does not connect** to anything following it. Copy and pronounce the word أولاد (*children*):

أولاد

Read aloud and copy the following names:

♀ داليا عَلْيا صالِحة دَلال خُلود جَليلة

♂ عَلي صالِح لَبيب خالِد جَلال جَعْفَر

Drill 8.

Dictation.

1. ____________ 6. ____________

2. ____________ 7. ____________

3. ____________ 8. ____________

4. ____________ 9. ____________

5. ____________ 10. ____________

Drill 9.

You will hear ten words. Circle the word you hear in each row:

1.	قَلْب	كِلاب	قَلَب	كَلب
2.	أذلّ	أطلّ	أظلّ	أضلّ
3.	عَقل	أكل	عِقال	عاقِل
4.	فَقر	فِكَر	فَكّر	فِقرة
5.	صَقَل	ثَكَل	شَكَل	تَكلّ
6.	رَقَص	رَكَض	رَفَس	رَكَل
7.	ذَرَف	صَرَف	ظَرف	شَرَف
8.	تَقدير	تَكدير	تَكرير	تَقرير
9.	حُزّي	خُذي	حوذي	خِزي
10.	بَلَغ	بَلَح	بَلَع	بَلَج

Drill 10.

Read the following advertisements. You will see a variation of ف : ڤ , which is sometimes used to indicate a *v* sound (Arabic has no letter for this sound).

1.

لصقة سالونبَاس أكوا - باتش

2.

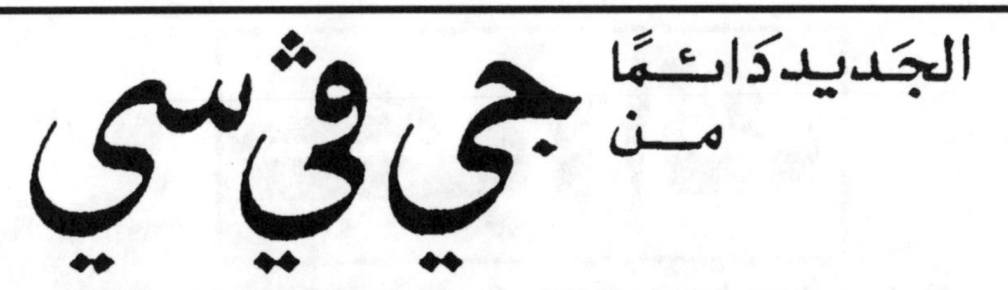

3.

4.

5.

باركلي ألـترا لايـتس

متعة متزايدة... وخفيفة، خفيفة!

6.

7.

١٢ حبة لبان
إنتاج : انكوجم ش.م.م
صنع في مصر
تشكلتس *
* بترخيص من شركة ورنر - لمبرت الولايات المتحدة
نكهة النعناع
تحتوي على : مادة لدنة ، سكر ، جلوكوز ، نشا ، وعطور طبيعية وصناعية

8.

9.

10.

من جريدة الشرق الاوسط ، ١٩٩٢

ء "hamza"

Thus far, you have seen hamza written on top of alif, أ , at the beginning of a word, and below alif, إ , when the initial vowel is kasra. You have also seen hamza written with no seat, ء , when it occurs at the end of a word after a long vowel. When hamza occurs in the middle of a word, it may be written on top of alif or rest on the line, as in the box above, **or** it may be written on one of the other long vowels: ؤ or ئ , depending on the surrounding long and short vowels. You will now learn the و and ى seats for the hamza.

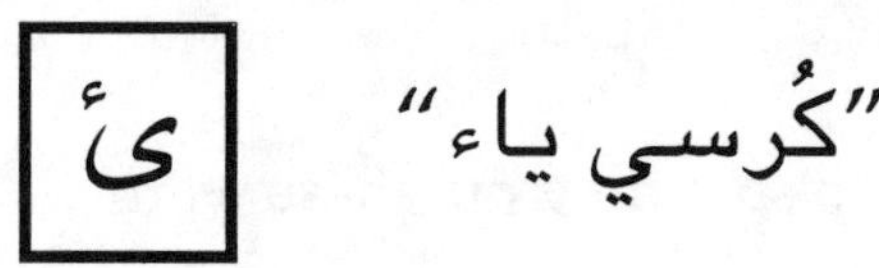

When hamza in the middle of a word is **preceded or followed by a kasra or long vowel** ي , it is written on a ى seat (كُرسي ياء). Notice that **when** ى **serves as a seat for hamza, it takes no dots.**

Listening Exercise 7.

Listen to the following words containing ئـ and repeat. Pay attention to the seat of the hamza and the vowels surrounding it:

طائِرة عائِشة خائِب قائِل أسئِلة قارِئ طوارِئ

Practice writing and reading ئـ by copying and sounding out these words:

ثائِر سُئِلَ طائِرات قَبائِل شاطِئ

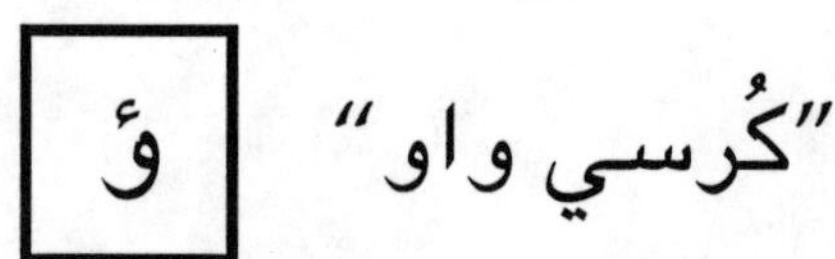

When hamza occurs in a word either preceded or followed by a Damma or long vowel و , it is written on a و seat (كُـرسـي واو) **as long as there is no kasra** (remember that, when preceded or followed by a kasra, hamza must be written as above, on ئـ).

Listening Exercise 8.

Listen to the following words containing ؤ and repeat. Notice the seat of hamza and the vowels surrounding it:

فُـؤاد سُـؤال رُؤوس رَؤوف بُـؤْس يُـؤْسِـف

Practice writing and reading ؤ by copying and sounding out these words:

تَـفاؤُل عَـشاؤُكَ أَصْـدِقـاؤُكَ يُـؤَثِّر

In other cases, that is, when medial hamza has only fatHa, alif, and/or sukuun, it is written on alif, as you learned earlier. The rules for writing hamza are rather complicated, so for now concentrate on recognizing these five seats of hamza when you see them. The best way to learn to write hamza correctly is to learn the spelling of words containing hamza one by one.

Drill 11.

You will hear one word of the three in each row. Circle the one you hear:

1.	زأر	زار	ذعر
2.	فرع	قرع	فزع
3.	غلاب	كلاب	قلاب
4.	صورة	سورة	ثورة
5.	عرف	عرك	عرق
6.	خائب	غائب	عائب
7.	تفاؤل	تفاعل	تفاءل
8.	سعل	سأل	شعل
9.	قباب	كباب	ضباب
10.	سائر	ثائر	شاعر
11.	سر	صر	زر
12.	قبس	كبس	جبس

Drill 12.

Fill in the long and short vowels and any shaddas that you hear:

1. ز — قـ — ق
2. قـ — بـ — س
3. قـ — و — ل
4. ط — يـ — ر
5. شـ — ر — ب
6. صـ — فـ — ف
7. يـ — كـ — بـ — ر
8. ضـ — يـ — ع
9. سـ — عـ — د
10. كـ — تـ — ب
11. ثـ — غـ — ر
12. ضـ — ر — ر —
13. يـ — شـ — تـ — ر —
14. شـ — ر — ع
15. ر — قـ — ب
16. صـ — عـ — ب

Drill 13.

Fill in the consonant that you hear in each of the following :

1.	تَـــــقيد	8.	صـــــير
2.	ـــــرْفـة	9.	ـــــديق
3.	ـــــيْف	10.	شَـخْـــــيّة
4.	فُـــــور	11.	ـــــريف
5.	ـــــقارِب	12.	ـــــحِكَت
6.	تَـــــليل	13.	تَـــــبُل
7.	ـــــابِق	14.	ـــــجر

Drill 14.

Read these phrases aloud:

طَبْخ طازَج	وَظيفة ثابِتة	عُكّازات طِبّيّة
ضَباب شَديد	رَغْبة قَوِيّة	طائِرات حَديثة
قَواعِد صَعْبة	رَجُل جَزائِريّ	تَراجُع وَتَخاذُل
أَسْئِلة ذَكِيّة	عِلاج طَبيعِيّ	أَحْصِنة سَريعة
لا يا سَعْدِيّة !	حِكاية قَصيرة	أَخْبار غَير سارّة
تَذاكِر غالِية	تَفاؤُل كَبير	سِفارات عَرَبِيّة
رَأْي قاطِع	فَصل طَويل	كتاب "أَلْف لَيْلة وَلَيْلة"

DRILL 15.

Connect the letters to form words, then listen to them on tape and write in the short vowels you hear:

1. ________________ = ت + س + ا + ؤ + ل

2. ________________ = ظ + ر + و + ف + ي

3. ________________ = و + ظ + ي + ف + ة

4. ________________ = أ + ك + ل + ا + ت

5. ________________ = غ + ر + ا + ئ + ب

6. ________________ = ج + ح + ا + ف + ل

7. ________________ = ف + و + ا + ئ + د

8. ________________ = أ + ف + ر + ي + ق + ي + ا

9. ________________ = خ + ل + ي + ف + ة

10. ________________ = ض + ر + و + ر + ا + ت

11. ________________ = أ + ظ + ا + ف + ر + ي

DRILL 16.

Dictation.

1. ________________ 6. ________________

2. ________________ 7. ________________

3. ________________ 8. ________________

4. ________________ 9. ________________

5. ________________ 10. ________________

Drill 17.

Read and learn these **nouns**:

طالِب — طالِبة

كُرسي — طاوِلة

كِتاب — شَريط

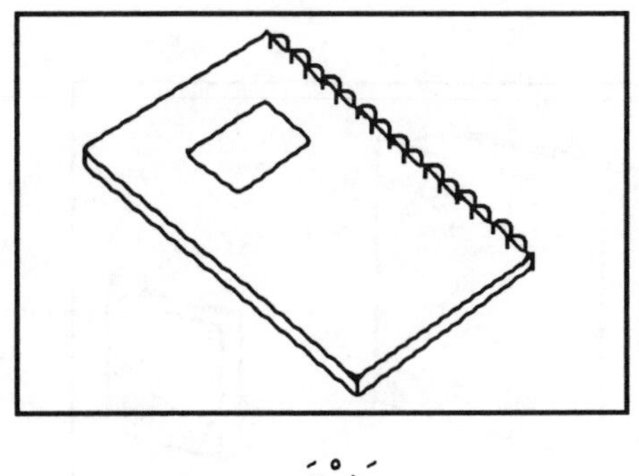

دَفْتَر

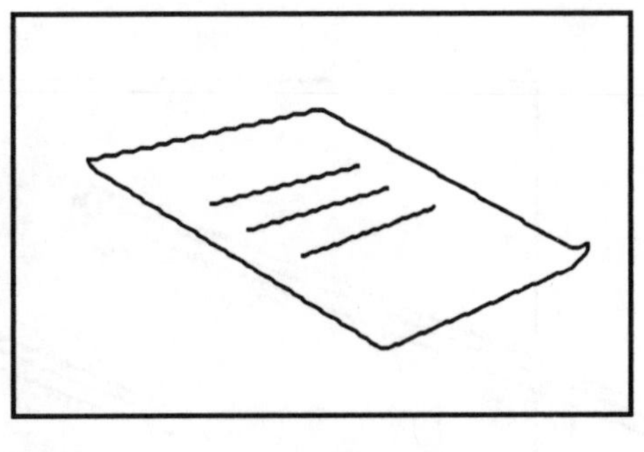

وَرَقة

فَصْل (صَفّ)

شُبّاك

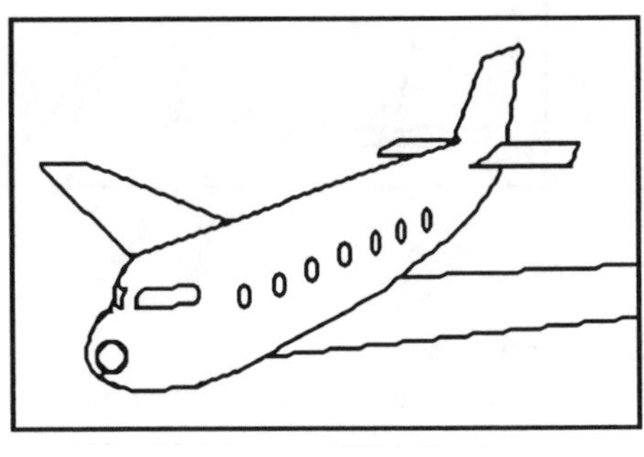

طائِرة

فُلوس

Now read and learn the following **adjectives:**

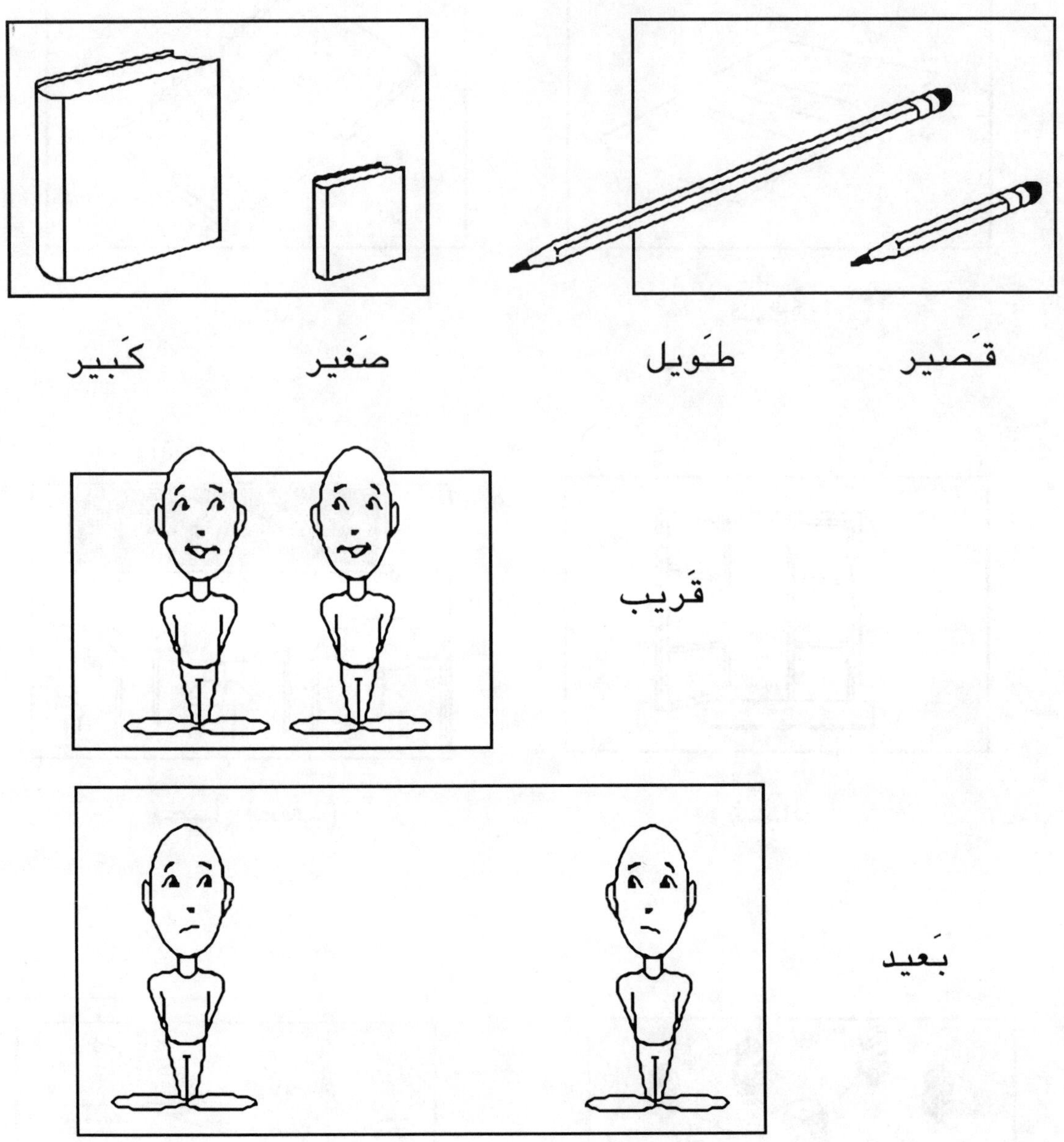

Drill 18.

How many phrases can you form with the words you know? Write them out.

Culture الثقافة

Video

Watch Scenes 12 and 13 with your teacher.

Coffee

Coffee and tea are the most popular social drinks in the Arab world. They are served to visitors at home and in the workplace, and men gather to drink them in coffeehouses. The choice between coffee and tea is partly a matter of local custom and supply, and partly a matter of personal taste. In much of North Africa, tea is more common, and is often made with loose green tea and mint, and drunk very sweet. In restaurants, coffee is usually served European style.

In Egypt and the Levant, Arabic coffee (also called Turkish coffee) is a strong drink made from very finely ground, dark beans, boiled in a little pot, and often served in demitasse cups or glasses. In Egypt, unless you request otherwise, coffee will be served to you *maZbuuT*, which means *just right*, referring to the amount of sugar (about one teaspoon per small cup). Tea is also popular, and served sweet.

In the Arabian Peninsula, another kind of Arabic coffee is served. The coffee beans are roasted in a different manner, and the coffee itself is almost clear in color and has a unique flavor. It is served in tiny cups without handles, and the cup is refilled by the host until the guest signals that he or she has had enough by tilting it from side to side several times.

Coffeehouses are popular meeting places, although by custom, they are frequented more by men than women in most Arab countries (women tend to socialize in their houses for privacy). In addition to coffee, tea, and other hot drinks, games such as chess and backgammon are available.

الوحدة السابعة

UNIT SEVEN

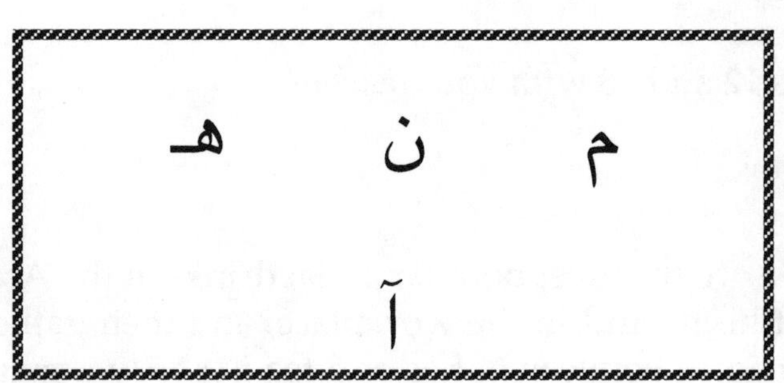

In this unit, you will learn the last three letters of the alphabet and the symbol *madda.*

م "miim"

This letter corresponds to English *m* as in *may.*

Listening Exercise 1.
Listen and repeat:

مال سَمير مِصْر جامِعة يَـوْم كَلام

Writing

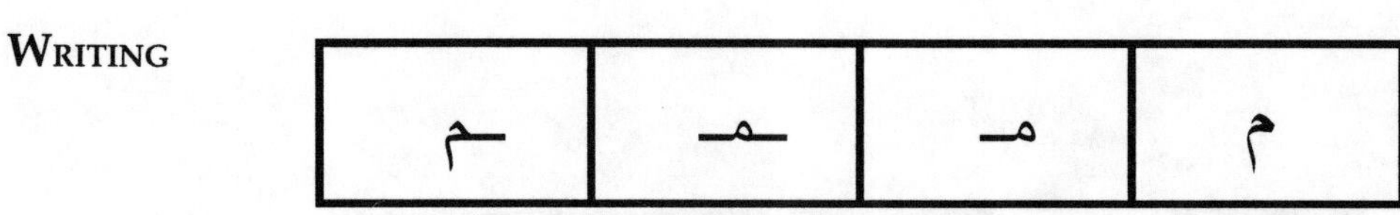

م is a connecting letter whose basic shape is easily identifiable: a small round loop. You can see from the words above that the printed forms do not vary much; however, the way the loop is drawn and connected to other letters varies in handwriting. It is important that you practice the direction of the loop in each position until you can write it easily, without having to stop and check.

To write independent م , begin on the line and draw a small round loop over and around to the right, continue along the line a short distance, then make a corner and draw the tail straight down well below the line. Copy:

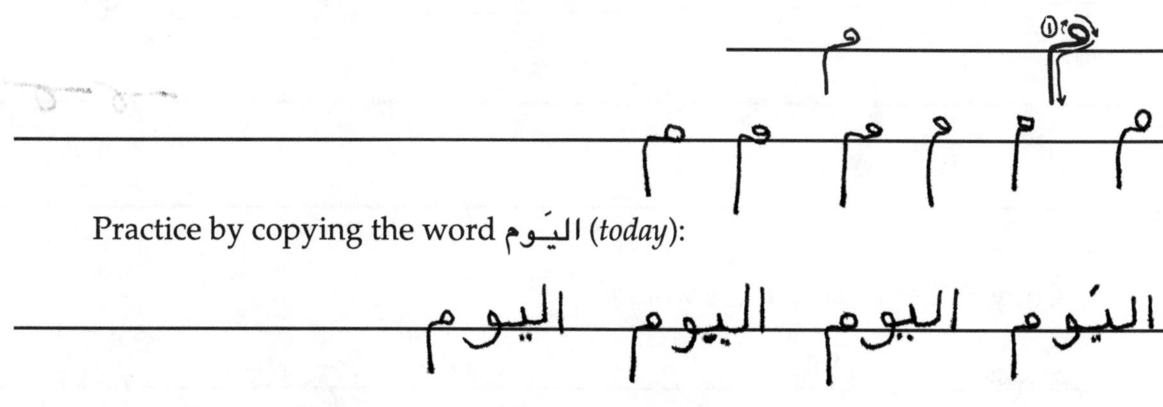

Practice by copying the word اليَوم (*today*):

There are two common styles of writing initial مـ . It may be looped up and over, just like independent م , or looped from underneath, in the opposite direction. Once you have closed the loop, continue on into a connecting segment. Copy and practice both examples, then choose one form to use:

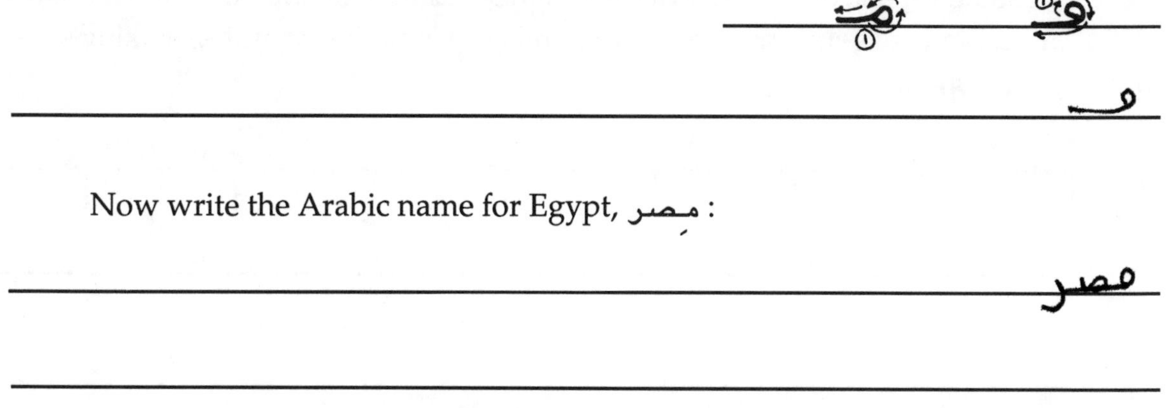

Now write the Arabic name for Egypt, مِصر :

When writing initial مـ followed by ج , ح , or خ , remember to draw the loop well above the line so that you can continue directly into the next letter. Copy the name مَجيد :

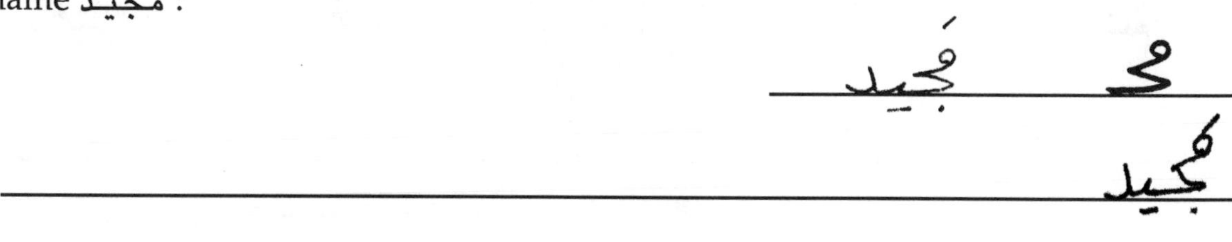

Medial ـمـ should **always loop down** from the connecting segment, which rests slightly above the line as the example shows:

Copy and sound out these words:

مال جامع يَعمَل قَمَر كَلام صَمّام

In some typefaces and handwriting styles, ـم may be joined to **initial** letters بـ ، تـ ، ثـ ، يـ , and مـ as shown: بم ، تم ، يم , and مم . Copy the examples, making sure to loop the م **down**:

مم مم يم يم تم تم بم بم

Read aloud and copy:

مُمتاز مُمِلّ يَميل بِم تَمام

When م follows an unconnected ل , it is usually written in the corner formed when ـا meets the line as shown. Copy the example:

Be on the lookout for this لـ combination in print. Copy and sound out:

أَلمَغرِب أَلماس أَلمَكسيك إلمام لَمّا

In handwriting, final ـم must be looped **down** from the top. Starting from the connecting segment, continue into the loop, then circle down and around to the right, making a full loop, then continue into the tail. Follow the arrows and practice:

Read and copy:

سالِم حَليم كَريم جيم ميم

Drill 1.

Dictation.

1. ______ 5. ______

2. ______ 6. ______

3. ______ 7. ______

4. ______ 8. ______

Copy and read aloud the following names:

♀ أمَل ماجِدة حَميدة جَميلة مَيّ كَريمة

♂ سامِر أحمَد مَحمود عِماد مَعروف عِصام

ن "nuun"

This letter represents the sound *n* as in *noon*.

Listening Exercise 2.

Listen and repeat:

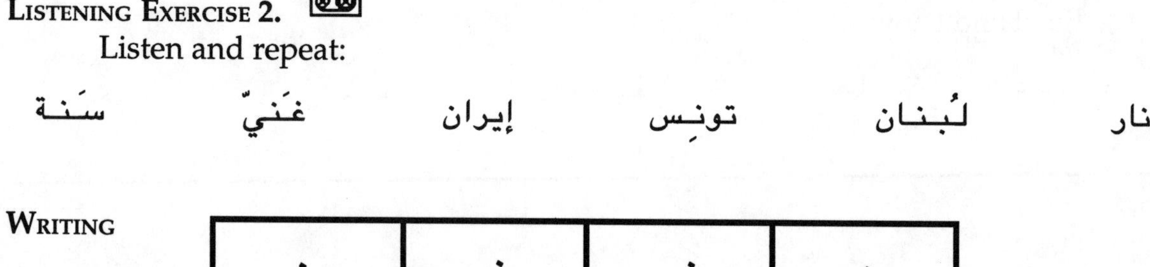

نار لُبنان تونِس إيران غَنيّ سَنة

Writing

ن	نـ	ـنـ	ـن

ن is a connecting letter whose shape resembles that of ب in initial and medial positions, except for the placement of the dot. It differs from ب in that the independent and final forms of ن take a characteristic "tail" shape that dips well below the line. Practice drawing the shape of independent ن , making sure to **bring the tail back up across the line:**

At the beginning or in the middle of a word, write ـنـ as you write ـبـ , but dot above rather than below the letter. Copy:

Read aloud and copy:

نَبي   نَبيل   تونِس   عِندي

In final position, ـن begins with a tooth and then dips immediately into a tail below the line. Bring the tail back up **across the line**:

Read and copy:

نون   لُبْنان   أَيْمَن   وَطَن

Now read aloud and copy the following names:

♀ زَيْنَب   إيمان   نَفيسة   نَجاة   حَنان   أماني

♂ أمين   ناجي   جُبران   مُنذِر   عَدنان   رَمَضان

Drill 2.

Read aloud these names of countries and cities:

عَمّان	نيويورك	فَرَنْسا	باريس
كولومبيا	بَغْداد	بَنغلاديش	كَنَدا
أَلْمانيا	موسكو	إفْريقيا	أَمْريكا
سورِيا	دِمَشق	بَيْروت	لُنْدُن
طَرابُلُس	أوسْتراليا	باكِستان	قَطَر
أفْغانِسْتان	بريطانْيا	موريتانْيا	صَنْعاء

Drill 3.

Dictation.

1. ______________________
2. ______________________
3. ______________________
4. ______________________
5. ______________________
6. ______________________
7. ______________________
8. ______________________
9. ______________________
10. ______________________

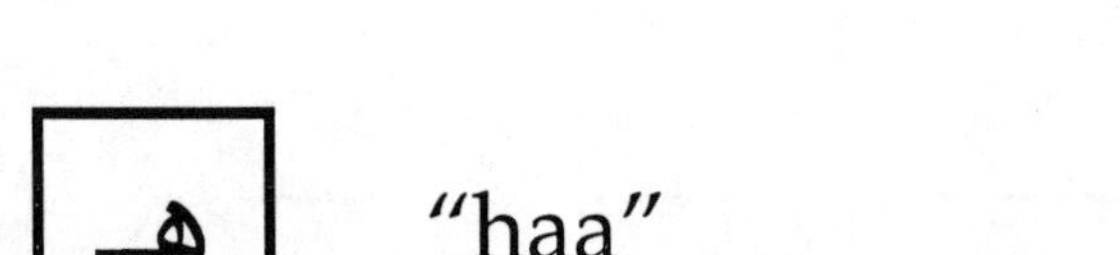

This letter represents a familiar sound, the one spelled in English by *h* as in *house*. Unlike English *h*, which can be silent, as in *hour* , ـهـ is always pronounced. Moreover, the English *h* sound tends to occur at the beginning of a word or syllable, whereas Arabic ـهـ can occur in any position. Say *a house* , then say the two words as if they were a single word. This is how ـهـ sounds in the middle of a word. Now say *her*, then say it backwards, pronouncing the *h*. This is how ـه sounds at the end of a word.

Listening Exercise 3.

Listen to the words on tape and repeat, paying attention to the هـ sound.

هَمْزة   ذَهَب   ظُهْر   نَهْر   يَتيه   بَناه

Writing

ه	ـه	ـهـ	هـ

The forms of this connecting letter vary more than those of any other. In addition, individual style may affect its shape in initial and medial forms. The shape هـ is the form this letter takes independently and at the beginning of a word. To write this shape, begin slightly above the line, and draw a large loop sloping first upward and then downward to your right and back up. This outer loop should be large; its exact shape can vary according to individual style and print type from a more pointed to a more rounded oval. When you reach the beginning of the loop, continue on, making a small loop inside the big one, then continue on down to the line into the connecting segment. Copy the example:

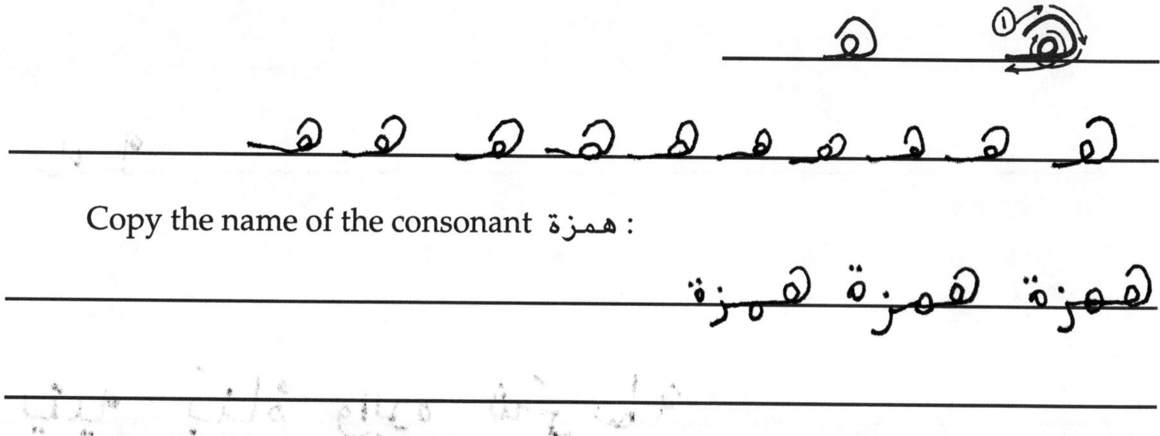

Copy the name of the consonant هَمزة :

In medial position, هـ has two main variations. The first is more common in print: ـهـ (look also at the printed form of the words in Listening Exercise 3 above); it consists of two vertical loops, one above and one below the line. The second is more commonly found in handwriting, and is written in one stroke as a (more or less) pointed dip below the line. Copy the example:

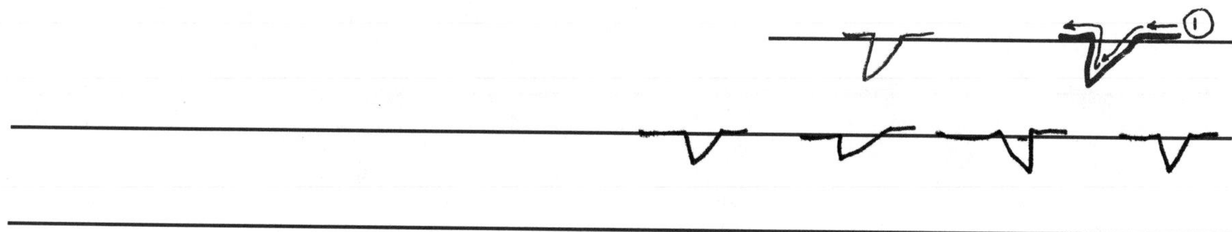

Copy and sound out the name مَها :

Final ـه takes the same shape as ـة (تاء مـربـوطـة), whether or not connected with a previous letter, **except that it has no dots. It is important to distinguish between these two letters:** while ـة is generally a feminine marker, ـه often indicates the possessive *his*. To write unconnected final ه , simply start above the line and draw a fat oval, just as you drew ة :

To write final ـه connected with a previous letter, start from the connecting segment and draw a short line up, then loop around into a flat oval. The exact shape of this oval varies according to individual style and print type. Copy:

To practice writing ه and ـه , copy and sound out:

يَتيه بَناهُ والِدُهُ شَريطَهُ

Now copy and sound out the following names:

♀ هَناء هِيام سُهَيْلة سُهَيْر زَهْرة

♂ هَيْثَم فَهْد هانـي سُهَيْل بَهاء

Drill 4. [tape]

Listen to the words on tape, decide whether the final letter you hear is ة or ه , and write it in the blank. Also write in all the short vowels that you hear:

1.	أبا ___	5.	دراسـ ___
2.	ميا ___	6.	دكتورا ___
3.	مدينـ ___	7.	في بيتـ ___
4.	كتبـ ___	8.	جميلـ ___

Remember that هـ is very different from ح . هـ is a sound that exists in English, and is very easy for English speakers to pronounce, while ح is pronounced deep in the throat, and has a slightly raspy sound. You can say هـ without thinking about your throat muscles, but you must concentrate to say ح . It is very important to distinguish between these two sounds, so practice until you can do so.

Listening Exercise 4. [tape]

Listen to the contrast between هـ and ح in the following pairs of words:

نَهْر / نَحْر   هُبوب / حُبوب   هَل / حَل   هَمزة / حَمزة

نَهَل / نَحَل   أبهَر / أبحَر   فَهْم / فَحْم   بَلَه / بَلَح

Drill 5. [tape]

You will hear twelve words . For each, circle the sound you hear:

1.	هـ	ح	5.	هـ	ح	9.	هـ	ح
2.	هـ	ح	6.	هـ	ح	10.	هـ	ح
3.	هـ	ح	7.	هـ	ح	11.	هـ	ح
4.	هـ	ح	8.	هـ	ح	12.	هـ	ح

Drill 6.

Read the following aloud with the tape, paying particular attention to ح and هـ :

1. (a)	حَول	(b)	هَول	7. (a)	أحرَقَ	(b)	أهرَقَ
2. (a)	حَمَد	(b)	هَمَد	8. (a)	مُبحِر	(b)	مُبهِر
3. (a)	شَحْم	(b)	شَهْم	9. (a)	ناحِية	(b)	ناهِية
4. (a)	جُحود	(b)	جُهود	10. (a)	اِستِحلال	(b)	اِستِهلال
5. (a)	حافي	(b)	هافي	11. (a)	إفحام	(b)	إفهام
6. (a)	طَحَل	(b)	طَهَل	12. (a)	أصحَرَ	(b)	أصهَرَ

Drill 7.

Write the letter that you hear in each blank:

1.	رَــــبة	5.	لِــــاف	9.	أـــم
2.	فـــيم	6.	ظُــــور	10.	ــــثالة
3.	جَبَــــات	7.	ــــريّة	11.	مشــــور
4.	ضاــــك	8.	صَــــراء	12.	ــــمّام

Drill 8.

Dictation.

1. ____________ 5. ____________

2. ____________ 6. ____________

3. ____________ 7. ____________

4. ____________ 8. ____________

آ "أَلِف مَدّة"

The symbol that you see above the alif in the box is called *madda,* مَدّة , which means *lengthening*. It can only occur on alif, and when it does, the alif is called alif madda, ألف مَدّة . The alif madda represents the combination of either أ + أ **or** ا + أ **.** These two combinations are never written separately, for the same historical reason that hamza is written on different seats: when Arabic was first written, hamza was not yet a part of the script. Only later was a symbol developed for hamza. The madda was also added to the alphabet with the other extra-alphabetical markings to indicate the two combinations above.

So far, you have learned five ways of writing hamza, depending on its position in a word and the vowels around it. Whenever two hamzas occur together, or hamza is followed by long vowel alif (as opposed to hamza followed by a short vowel), rather than writing أأ or أا , the combination is written as آ . This is pronounced as a hamza followed by alif. **Remember: Like medial and final hamza, the madda sign must be written wherever it occurs.**

LISTENING EXERCISE 5.

Listen and repeat:

آن　　آمين　　آكُل　　القُرآن　　الآن　　مِرآة

The مدّة sign written above the الف is written as a slightly wavy line just above it. Copy the example:

Practice writing madda in القُرآن (*the Quran*):

Drill 9.

Connect the following letters to form words, then listen to them on tape and write in the vowels you hear:

1. ____________________	=	أ + ن + هـ + ا + ر
2. ____________________	=	ك + ر + ي + م
3. ____________________	=	م + ذ + ا + هـ + ب
4. ____________________	=	ط + م + ا + ط + م
5. ____________________	=	ن + هـ + ا + ي + ا + ت
6. ____________________	=	ك + ل + ا + م + هـ
7. ____________________	=	أ + أ + ك + ل + هـ + ا
8. ____________________	=	ك + هـ + ر + ب + ا + ء
9. ____________________	=	ت + ع + ظ + ي + م
10. ____________________	=	غ + ف + ر + ا + ن
11. ____________________	=	أ + س + ئ + ل + ة

Drill 10.

A. Read aloud these names of Middle Eastern foods:

فَلافِل	أُمّ عَلي	تَبّولة	بابا غَنّوج
حُمُّص	فَتّة	فَتّوش	وَرَق عِنَب
مَحْشي	كُبّة	كَباب	لَبَن زَبادي
مُلوخِيّة	بامْية	كُسْكسو	مَقْلوبة
كُنافة	بَقْلاوة	بَسْبوسة	طَحينة

B. Now read and learn the names of some other foods:

قَـهْوة عربـيّة (تُركيّة)

قـهـوة أمـريكيّة

شاي

حَليب (لَبَن)

ماء

سُكَّر

خُـبْـز

خُـبْـز عَرَبي

Drill 11.

Read and learn the following words:

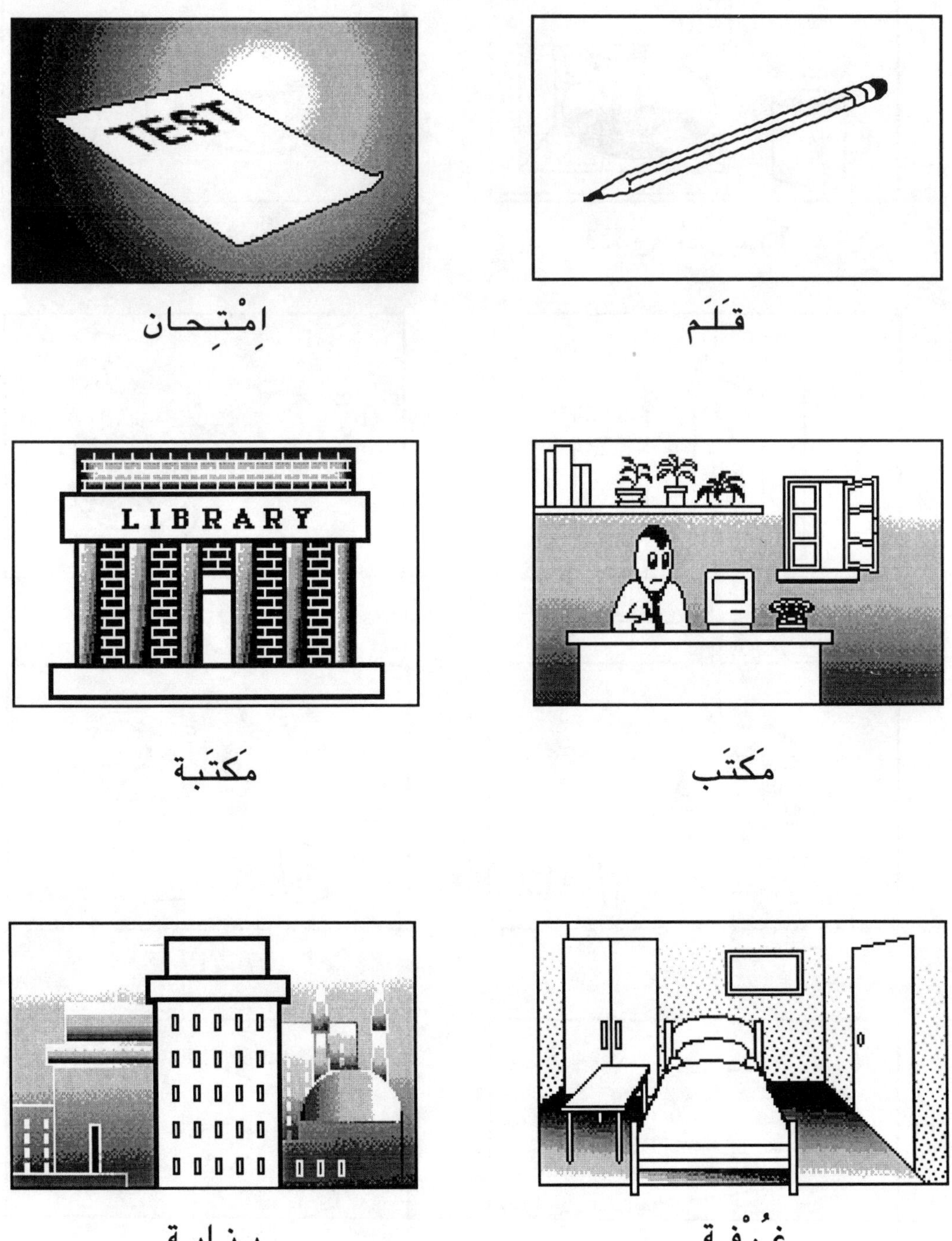

قَلَم — اِمْتِحان

مَكتَب — مَكتَبة

غُرْفة — بِناية

Drill 12.

You are now ready to play your first Arabic word game, taken from an Arabic newspaper. In the box below, look for the words listed in the two columns to the right, running in any direction. Once you find the word, circle it or draw a line through it. After you have found all the words, write out the remaining unused letters. They will spell the name of a famous Biblical/Quranic prophet.

الكلمة الضائعة

ج	ن	ق	ص	ا	ن	م	ع	د
ف	س	ج	ف	ر	ش	ي	ع	ا
ا	ع	و	و	س	ح	ص	ا	ن
ف	ي	ف	ا	ا	ف	ي	ن	ز
ك	د	م	ج	و	ع	ا	ب	س
ع	ح	ة	ر	ق	ي	ب	و	ب
ك	ظ	ي	غ	ز	و	س	ب	ك
ض	ع	ي	ف	ر	ن	ة	ف	و
ز	ي	ا	د	ة	ن	أ	ش	ك

عصفور	زيادة
عيون	يابسة
انبوب	ضعيف
زناد	سامح
رزق	كعك
كوكب	حاجة
جوف	نقصان
جفاف	غيظ
شرف	شأن
عم	سعيد

الحل السابق	الكلمة الضائعة
صنافير	من الانبياء

من جريدة الشرق الاوسط، ١٩٩٢

Drill 13.

Read and learn the following words that express how you feel:

إزّيك؟ / كَيف الحال؟

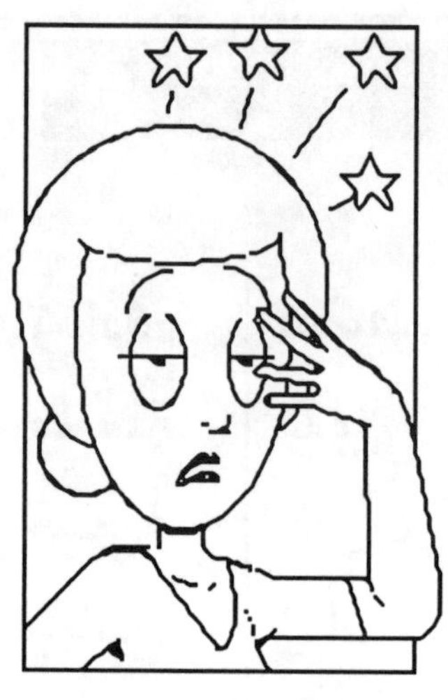

عندي صُداع

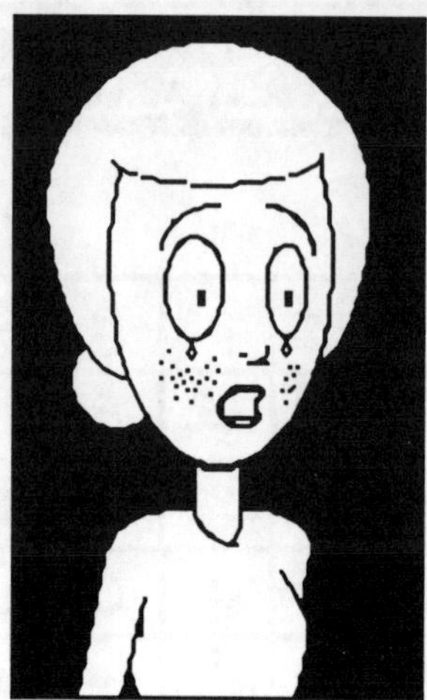

زَعْلانة

كوَيِّسة ، الحَمْدُ لِلّه

غَضْبان

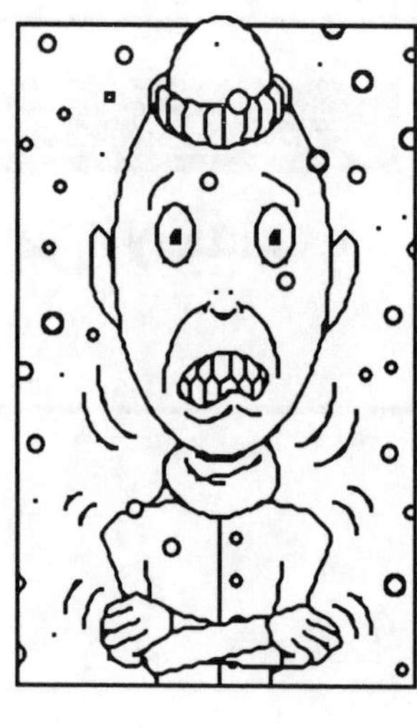

بَرْدان

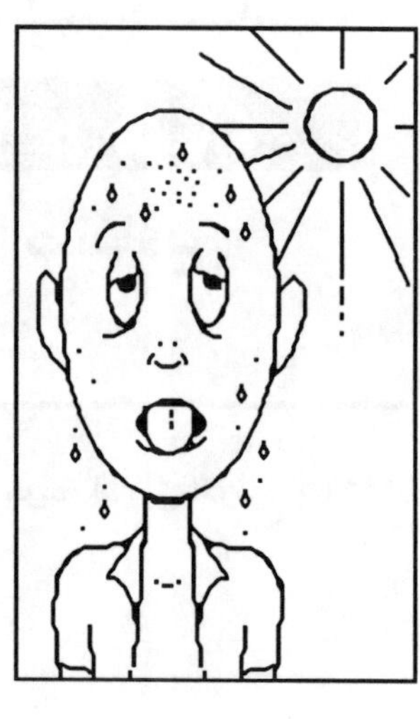

حَرّان

عنْدي بَرد

مَريض

جَوعان

تَعبانة

عَطشان

أنا	I	هُوَ	he
أنْتَ	you (masculine)	هِيَ	she
أنْتِ	you (feminine)	نَعَم / لا	yes / no

Drill 14.

Read the following advertisements and write them out in your own handwriting:

1.

2.

بولو شيرت

١٠٠٪ قطن مصري

صنع في مصر

3.

سامسونج

4.

ميتسوبيشي اليكتريك

5.

6.

هوليدي إن

الرياض

أمسية سندباد

7.

8.

9.

10.

11.

جنرال اليكتريك
كنت
لايتس
جديدة
دايهاتسو
ميشلان
الأمان مع الزمان
دجاج كنتاكي
ساندوتش
الدجاج
الجديد
طعمها لا يقاوم!

12.

13. فولكس واجن

14. مرسيدس 230E

15. تكساس إنسترومنتس

من جريدة الشرق الاوسط ، ١٩٩٢

CULTURE الثقافة 

 **VIDEO**

Watch Scene 14 on the video with your teacher.

"مَعْلِهْش"

The colloquial expression "مـَعلهش" (also spelled مـَعليش) has a wide range of usages. It is used to say *never mind, don't worry about it, it doesn't matter,* in some cases, to say *is it okay (if I...)?*, and, finally, to console someone who is upset or angry about something.

Some kinds of behavior that many Americans may see as interfering or speaking out of turn are quite acceptable in Arab culture. For example, when a person sees that someone is upset, he or she will probably try to find out what the problem is, and say معلهش —even if he or she does not know the person well.

معلهش!!

الوحدة الثامنة

UNIT EIGHT

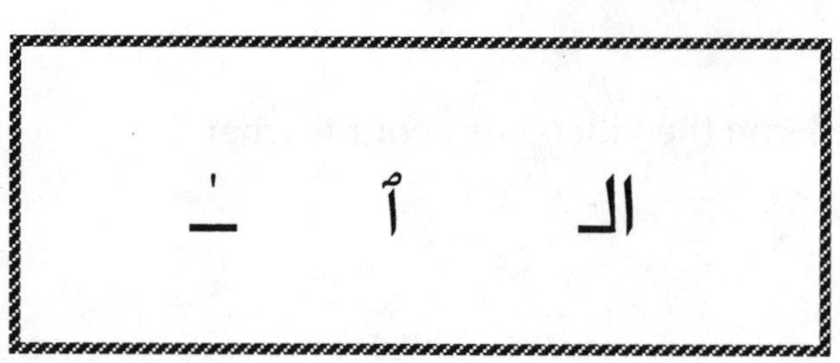

In this unit, you will learn about the definite article, more about initial hamza, and an old spelling for alif that still survives in a few words. You will also learn the numbers zero through ten.

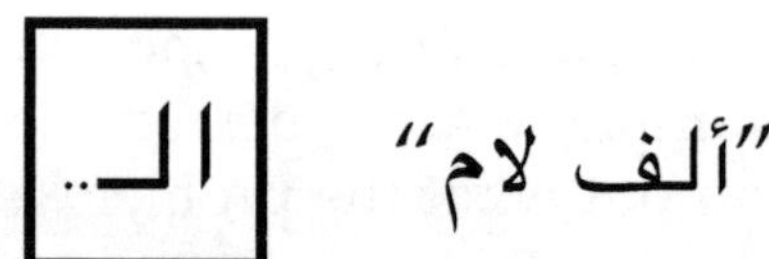

Called in Arabic ألف لام after the names of the letters, the segment الـ represents the definite article in Arabic, comparable to *the* in English. Compare the following pairs of nouns:

the book	الكتاب	*a book*	كتاب
the teacher	الاستاذ	*a teacher*	استاذ

You can see in these examples that الـ makes an indefinite noun definite. Of course, the usage of Arabic الـ is not exactly equivalent to that of English *the*. For example, you have already learned how to say:

جامعة القاهرة *The University of Cairo*

in which جامعة is definite although it does not have الـ (you will learn more about this soon). Proper nouns are definite whether or not they begin with الـ ; for example, مصر (*Egypt*) is definite. There is no rule that determines whether or not a proper noun takes الـ ; each one must be memorized (especially the names of Arab countries and cities). In general, however, foreign names and names of people do not usually take الـ . You will learn more about these differences over the next few weeks; in the meantime, remember that **a word modified by الـ is definite.**

Listening Exercise 1.

Read and listen to the following examples of words with and without ال .

1. البيت <= بيت   4. الأستاذة <= أستاذة

2. القلم <= قلم   5. المكتبة <= مكتبة

3. المكتب <= مكتب   6. الكرسي <= كرسي

Pronunciation of ال

ال has a special pronunciation rule which dictates that, before certain letters, ل is not pronounced as ل , but is elided to or "swallowed by" the following consonant. As a result, the following consonant takes a shadda and is pronounced as a doubled consonant because it has "swallowed" the sound of the ل while retaining its length. For example, the word الدكتور is pronounced *ad-duktuur* (**not** *al-duktuur*) because د is one of the letters that assimilates the ل of ال . The letters that assimilate this ل are called الحُروف الشّمسيّة (*sun letters*, pronounced *al-Huruuf ash-shamsiyya*), after the word شَمس (*sun*) which begins with ش , one of the letters that assimilates ل . The consonants that do not assimilate the ل are called الحُروف القَمَرية (*moon letters*, pronounced *al-Huruuf al-qamariyya*), because the ق of قَمَر (*moon*) is one of the letters that do not assimilate ل .

Listening Exercise 2.

Listen to the following examples of sun and moon letters and repeat. Pay close attention to the pronunciation of ال :

الحروف القمرية : البيت القلم الاستاذ الكتاب الأوتوبيس

الحروف الشمسية : الشّارع السّيّارة الصّفّ الطّاولة الطّائرة

Note that the first group of words contains the sound ل , whereas in the second, you do not hear ل , but rather a shadda on the following consonant. This shadda is sometimes written in, as it is above, as a reminder of correct pronunciation. In fully vocalized texts, it is considered part of proper vowelling, and will always be written in. It is a good idea to write the shadda on الحروف الشمسية for now, until you have memorized them and remember to read ال correctly.

The following chart lists the letters in their proper classes. As a rule of thumb, note that الحروف الشمسية —the letters that swallow the ل —are the ones whose tongue position is close to that of ل . This rule will help you **memorize** which group each letter belongs to so that you can speak and read Arabic correctly:

الـ + الحُروف الشَمسيّة والحُروف القَمَريّة

الحروف الشمسية	الحروف القمرية
ت	أ
ث	ب
د	ج
ذ	ح
ر	خ
ز	ع
س	غ
ش	ف
ص	ق
ض	ك
ط	م
ظ	هـ
ل	و
ن	ي

Drill 1.

Make these indefinite words definite by adding الـ , write شـدة on those that begin with حروف شمسية , and read aloud:

1. ______	جامعة	8. ______	سلام
2. ______	اِسم	9. ______	مدينة
3. ______	طالب	10. ______	أستاذة
4. ______	شريط	11. ______	كتاب
5. ______	فصل	12. ______	صباح
6. ______	قهوة	13. ______	درس
7. ______	ورقة	14. ______	باب

Drill 2.

Write شــدة on the حـروف شـمـسـيـة in the following words, and write سكون on the ـل before حروف قمرية, as in the examples. Then read the words aloud.

Examples: الْقُرآن الرّاديو

الدكتور	البيْت	المدينة	الطائرة	الشارع
الكَعبة	الصف	الديمُقراطي	القرآن	السيارة
اللَوح	العَيْن	الغَزال	السؤال	النَهر
الظَلام	الإسلام	الحِزب	الخَير	الثَقافة

Drill 3.

Circle the word you hear in each row. Pay special attention to the first syllable in each word and listen for the presence or absence of shadda on sun letters.

1.	أسلم	إسلام	السلام
2.	صفّ	الصفّ	أصفّ
3.	أعمل	عمل	العمل
4.	أنهاية	نهاية	النهاية
5.	أقلام	قلم	القلم
6.	صوم	أصوم	الصوم
7.	أصبح	الصباح	صباح
8.	الظلام	أظلم	ظلام
9.	ثاني	أثاني	الثاني
10.	نور	النور	أنور

Drill 4.

You will hear twelve words. Write ال for each word that contains it and Ø for each word that does not.

1. ________	4. ________	7. ________	10. ________
2. ________	5. ________	8. ________	11. ________
3. ________	6. ________	9. ________	12. ________

Drill 5.

You will hear eight phrases. Determine whether the **second** word in each is definite or indefinite, and write ال for those that are definite and Ø for those that are indefinite:

1. ________	3. ________	5. ________	7. ________
2. ________	4. ________	6. ________	8. ________

Drill 6.

Read aloud the following words:

البَحْرَين	الطّالِب	اللَّيلة	الخاصّ	الزِّيارة
الكُوَيت	الإمارات	النّيل	الدّار	الوَلَد
الضَّباب	الأُردُن	الحَليب	الفار	المَغرِب
الخَرْطوم	السّودان	الدَّوحة	الثّاني	الشُّبّاك
الغالي	الظَّلام	الذَّهاب	اليَمَن	الرَباط
الجَزائِر	التّونِسي	القلم	العِراق	الصّومال

Drill 7.

Dictation. Remember that you will not hear ل in ال on words that begin with حروف شمسية — **listen for shadda!**

1. ________________	5. ________________	9. ________________
2. ________________	6. ________________	10. ________________
3. ________________	7. ________________	11. ________________
4. ________________	8. ________________	12. ________________

أ "هَمْزة الوَصْل"

You have seen that words like أستاذ begin with the consonant هَمزة (whether or not it is written: ا or أ). It is the همزة that "allows" you to pronounce the vowel that follows it. In most words that begin with همزة , the vowel that the hamza carries always remains the same; for example, أستاذ is always pronounced the same way, with a ضَمّة . However, the همزة of الـ belongs to a special category called همزة الوَصل , which means *elidable hamza*. "Elidable" means that, when preceded by another word, the hamza and its vowel drop in both pronunciation and writing. In writing, the symbol *waSla* وَصلة takes the place of the همزة , and in pronunciation, the original vowel on the alif is swallowed by the final vowel of a previous word or by a helping vowel. Thus, in the case of الـ , the normal فَتحة vowel on the alif is not usually heard.

Listening Exercise 3.

Listen carefully to الـ in the second word of each phrase. You will not hear the ا of the الـ because it is swallowed by the final vowel of the preceding word:

أبي ٱلعزيز	أمريكا ٱللاتينية	في ٱلبيت	في ٱلجامعة
بيتي ٱلجديد	مدرّسو ٱلجامعة	والدا ٱلبنت	كرسي ٱلطالب

Writing

The symbol for همزة الوصل , called وَصلة , is not normally written except in completely vowelled texts. It can only occur at the beginning of a word, and the overwhelming majority of cases occur on الـ . Practice writing it by copying the example:

ٱلـ ٱلـ

Drill 8.

Listen as the following phrases are read aloud. Some will contain regular همزة and some will contain همزة الوصل . Mark **either** همزة **or** وصلة according to what you hear:

1.	ما اسمك ؟	6.	أينَ البيت ؟
2.	والدي استاذ	7.	هُوَ احمد
3.	عندي الم	8.	في المدينة
4.	لي اسنان	9.	أخو البنت
5.	صديقي الفرنسي	10.	أنا الاستاذ

ٰ dagger alif

This symbol is often called *dagger alif* because its shape resembles a small dagger. It represents an old spelling of alif from early Quranic writing that survives today in a few common words and names. It is pronounced exactly like the long vowel alif.

Listening Exercise 4.

Listen to these words containing dagger alif and repeat:

عَبد الرَّحمٰن　　الله　　لٰكِن　　هٰذا

Learn the following words:

but	لٰكِن	this (masculine)	هٰذا
God	اللّٰه	this (feminine)	هٰذِهِ

These are most of the commonly used words that are spelled with dagger alif. It is almost never written, except in fully vowelled texts, but is important to learn the words that are spelled with it and remember to **pronounce this as a long vowel—it is equivalent to alif.**

Writing

The dagger alif is drawn as a short vertical stroke above the consonant it follows. Make sure it is precisely vertical, so that it may be distinguished easily from the slanted fatHa. Copying the examples, practice writing and pronouncing the words you have just learned:

هٰذا هٰذا هٰذِهِ هٰذِهِ لٰكِن لٰكِن اللّٰه اللّٰه

Drill 9.

A. Read the following phrases aloud, paying special attention to همزة الوصل and الحروف الشمسية والقمرية :

في الشاي	مِنَ المَغرِب	مَعَ الخُبز
مِنَ المكتبة	أمامَ الطاولة	في هذا الشارع
في هٰذِهِ الجامعة	وَراءَ الباب	أمامَ الشبّاك
أمامَ الفصل	في هٰذا البيت	في هٰذِهِ البناية
مَعَ القهوة	مِنَ الكتاب	وَراءَ الجامعة
وَراءَ البِناية	هٰذا الأوتوبيس	في السيارة

B. Use the following prepositions to figure out the meanings of the phrases:

in في	*with* مَعَ
in front of أمام	*behind* وَراءَ

Drill 10.

Read the following passage, first to yourself, for meaning, then aloud. What does it seem to be talking about? How much can you understand?

اسمي عَلي مُحَمَّد عَبد السّلام. أنا عِراقي من مدينة بغداد وأنا طالب في جامعة بغداد. أنا ساكِن في شارع البَصرة. أبي أستاذ في الجامعة وَاسمُه محمد وأمي دكتورة واسمها عائِشة. عندي خمسة إخْوة: إبْراهيم وخَليل وحامِد وماجِدة وسامِية.

Drill 11.

Read the sentences below and learn the new words:

هذه بنْت
هذا ولَد
هذهِ اِمْرَأة
هذا رَجُل
هذه بنت جَميلة
beautiful
هذا طالب
هذا رجل قَصير
هذا رجل طَويل
هذه سيّارة صغيرة
هذه سيّارة كَبيرة

Drill 12.

Match the nouns and adjectives given below to form sentences using هذا and هذه . Remember that all the words in a sentence must have the same gender, either masculine or feminine.

Adjectives	Nouns	
قصير / قصيرة ≠ طويل / طويلة	كِتاب	قلم
صغير / صغيرة ≠ كبير / كبيرة	طاولة	رجل
جديد / جديدة ≠ قَديم / قديمة	شُبّاك	اِمرأة
قريب / قريبة ≠ بعيد / بعيدة	سيّارة	بنت
صعب / صعبة ≠ سَهل / سهلة	أوتوبيس	ولد
جميل / جميلة	طائرة	قهوة
عربي / عربيّة	صفّ	شاي
أمريكي / أمريكيّة	جامعة	مكتب
واسع / واسعة	مكتبة	غرفة
جَيِّد / جَيِّدة *(good)*	امتحان	بناية
طَيِّب / طَيِّبة *tasty (food), good (person)*	استاذ / ة	شارع

Example: هذه سيّارة جديدة

1. ______________
2. ______________
3. ______________
4. ______________
5. ______________
6. ______________
7. ______________
8. ______________
9. ______________
10. ______________
11. ______________
12. ______________
13. ______________
14. ______________
15. ______________
16. ______________

Arabic Numerals and Numbers

9	8	7	6	5	4	3	2	1	0
٩	٨	٧	٦	٥	٤	٣	٢	١	٠

The chart above shows two sets of numerals. Both are used in the Arab world: the set in the top row is used in the Arab west (Morocco, Algeria, and Tunisia), while the one in the bottom row is prevalent in the other Arab countries. The numerals used in the Arab west were introduced into Europe from Islamic lands in the Middle Ages—hence our name for them, Arabic numerals. We know that the Arabs adapted their numerals from India, but we do not know the exact history of the development of the two sets. One of the great Islamic contributions to mathematics was the introduction of zero, attributed to the great mathematician and astronomer al-Khawarizmi (d. A.D. 849), from whose name the word *logarithm* comes.

The numerals used in the Arab east are shown along with the Arabic names for numbers in the following table. Read and learn:

Counting Numbers from 0 to 10	
صِفْر	٠
واحِد	١
اِثنان / اِثْنَيْن [1]	٢
ثَلاثة	٣
أَرْبَعة	٤
خَمْسة	٥
سِتّة	٦
سَبْعة	٧
ثَمانِية	٨
تِسْعة	٩
عَشَرة	١٠

[1] اثنان and اثْنَيْن are variants; learn to recognize both. اثْنَيْن is more commonly used in spoken Arabic.

Most Arabic numerals appear in handwriting much the same way they appear in print, with the exception of ٢ and ٣ . In print, they appear as shown: ٢ , ٣ . In handwriting, however, they take on slightly different forms. Study the examples:

٢ = ٢

٣ = ٣

You can see that the numeral ٢ in print closely resembles the numeral ٣ when written by hand, except that the hook at the top of handwritten ٣ is usually deeper. To avoid confusion, always write these numerals as shown in the handwritten example above, and when reading, remember to differentiate between printed and handwritten forms.

Now practice writing the numerals by copying the examples:

١٠ ٩ ٨ ٧ ٦ ٥ ٤ ٣ ٢ ١ ٠

DRILL 13.

Quiz! Prepare five arithmetic problems for your classmates using the numbers 0 to 10. You can use the following expressions:

زائِد	+
ناقِص	–
في	×

Example: — خمسة زائد ثلاثة ؟

— ثمانية .

Drill 14.

Get the names and phone numbers of your classmates (in Arabic!) and write them below:

Telephone التلفون	Address العنوان	Name الاسم

Culture الثقافة

Video

Watch Scenes 15 and 16 with your teacher.

Saying Hello

You have learned that polite behavior requires you to say hello to anyone in a room you enter. The same principle also applies to a loosely defined "space" that someone regularly occupies, such as an outdoor work area, or a guard's position outside a building.

The following list includes the most frequently used greetings. Add them to your list of active vocabulary, and use them often:

to welcome someone to one's home or workplace	*(ahlan wa sahlan)*	أهلاً (وَسَهلاً)
to reply:		أهلاً بِك
in the morning, until lunch time		صَباح الخَير
to reply:		صَباح النّور
in the late afternoon or evening		مَساء الخَير
to reply:		مَساء النّور
common in Lebanon, Syria, Palestine, Jordan	*(marHaban)*	مَرحَبا / مَرحَبًا
to reply:		أهلاً / مَرحبتَيْن
"Islamic" in connotation		السّلامُ عَلَيْكُم
to reply:		وَعَلَيْكُمُ السّلام

الوحدة التاسعة

UNIT NINE

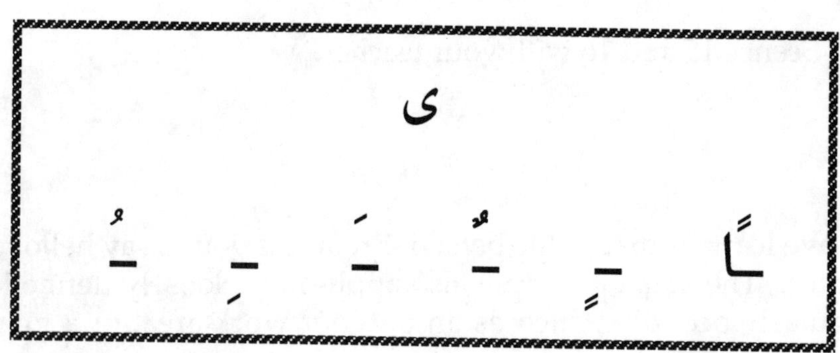

In this unit you will learn the third spelling of alif, and the symbols that represent grammatical endings. **All of these symbols can occur only at the end of a word.**

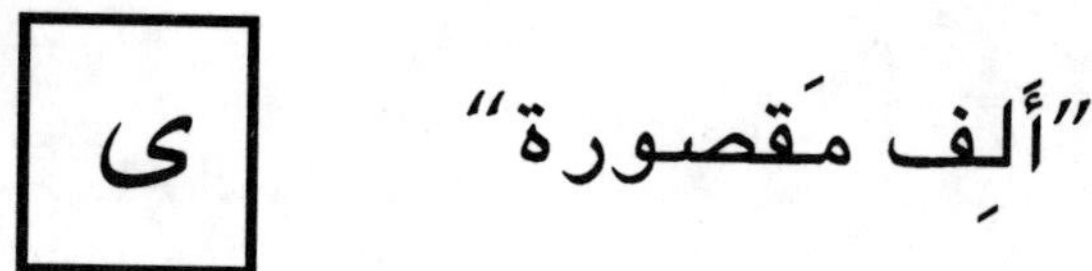

Alif maqSuura, also called ألف بصـورة اليـاء , *alif in the shape of yaa'*, is a variant spelling of alif that **can only occur at the end of a word.** This shape of alif is a spelling convention that dates back to the writing of the Quran. **It is pronounced just like the regular alif.** When the long vowel alif occurs at the end of a word, it is often spelled with alif maqSuura, unless the word is a proper noun, in which case it is usually written with a regular alif.

LISTENING EXERCISE 1.

Listen to the following examples of words ending in ألف مقصورة and repeat:

عَلى   إلى   مَشى   بَكى   اِنْتَهى   مُثَنّى

Writing

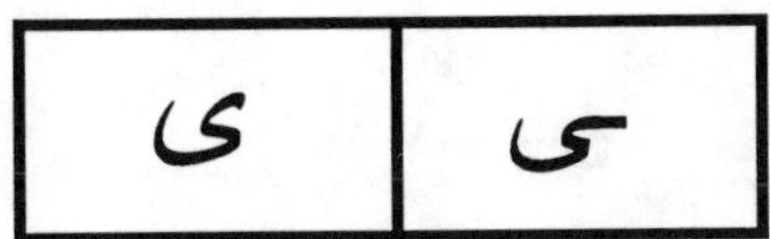

ى is a connector, and since it only occurs in final position, it has only the two shapes you see above. It is written exactly like final ي , **except that it has no dots.** In other words, final ي and ى are distinguished by the two dots of the ي, **except in Egypt, where both are usually written without dots.** Copy the example:

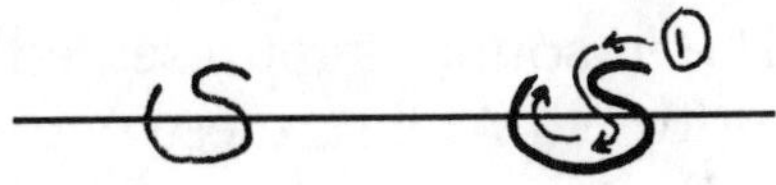

Copy and read aloud the following female names that end in ى:

لَيْلى　　مُنى　　سَلمى　　نَجوى　　نُهى

Drill 1.

Read the following phrases aloud. **Remember to elide the همزة الوصل** :

١- مُسْتَشْفى السَّلام　　٥- مَغْزى الكَلام　　٩- صُغْرى أَخَواتِها

٢- مَقْهى الشَّباب　　٦- هٰذِهِ أكبَر بَلْوى　　١٠- السَّنة الأُولى

٣- نَهْر بَرَدى　　٧- شَكوى ثانية　　١١- بِدون مَأْوى

٤- بريطانيا العُظمى　　٨- حَلْوى لَذيذة　　١٢- اِسمُها نُهى

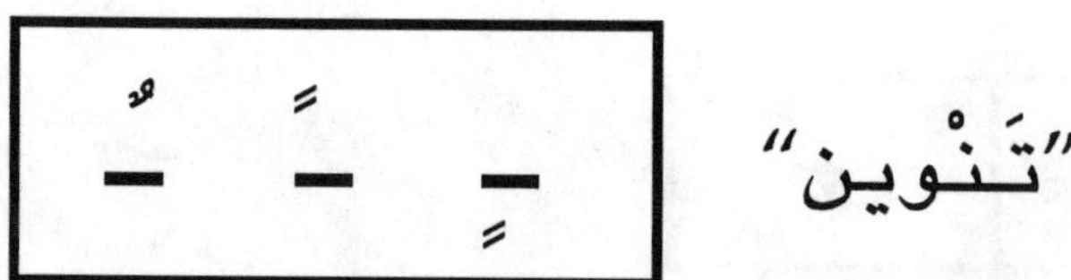

"تَنْوين"

The word *tanwiin*, derived from the name of the letter نون , refers to the *n* sound in these three endings:

ـٌ (pronounced *un*)   ـً (pronounced *an*)   ـٍ (pronounced *in*)

The *n* sound is represented in writing by the doubling of the short vowel symbol. In formal Arabic, these endings occur on **indefinite** nouns and adjectives, and they indicate certain grammatical functions of words in a sentence. Except in very formal situations, such as public addresses, they are rarely used in speaking, and are only written in vowelled texts. They are for the most part superfluous to comprehension, since speech and normal prose rely on other grammatical devices, such as word order, to convey meaning. For the time being, you need not worry about their meanings; you are expected to recognize them simply as "grammatical endings" when you hear them.

Note that the ة *taa marbuuTa* is pronounced ت before *tanwiin*, as you will hear in the following exercise.

LISTENING EXERCISE 2.

Listen to the following words being read with each tanwiin ending.

سيّارةٌ / سيارةً / سيارةٍ   رجلٌ / رجلاً / رجلٍ   اِمرأةٌ / امرأةً / امرأةٍ

Whether you hear *an*, *in*, or *un*, the meaning of each of these words remains the same: *a car*, *a man*, and *a woman*, respectively. We will now take a brief look at each of these endings in turn.

ـً "تـنوين الفَتْح"

This ending, pronounced *an*, may be found on indefinite nouns and adjectives. Of the three tanwiin endings, it is the only one you will see in unvowelled texts, and the only one used in everyday speech. You have already learned several words that end in تنوين الفتح.

LISTENING EXERCISE 3.

Read these familiar words that end in تنوين الفتح and repeat, noting the spelling:

شُكرًا   عَفوًا   مَرحَبًا   أهلاً   أهلاً وسهلاً

WRITING

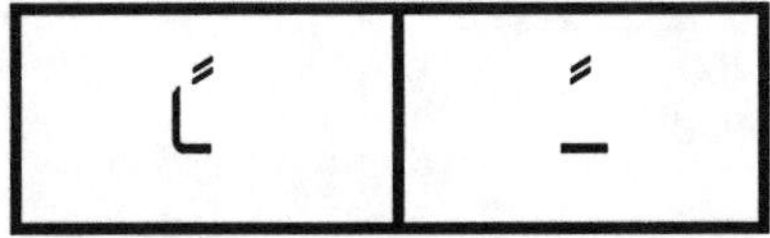

As you can see in the box above, تنوين الفتح has two different written forms. The form on the right, a double fatHa, is used on words that end in ة and اء (alif followed by hamza). The form on the left, in which تنوين الفتح rests on an alif seat, is used in most other cases. Compare the spelling of the words in row A to that of the words in B:

A   ساعةً   استاذةً   مساءً   سماءً

B   شُكرًا   عَفوًا   جِدًّا   أهلاً

Like other short vowel markings, the double fatHa in تنوين الفتح is not normally written in unvocalized texts. **However, the alif seat that represents تنوين الفتح is always written where required,** which means that alif at the end of a word usually represents تنوين الفتح rather than a long vowel. Compare the vocalized words in row B above to the same words, unvocalized this time, in row C below:

C   شكرا   عفوا   جدا   اهلا

The function of final alif as a seat for تنوين الفتح may be easily distinguished from the vowel alif because, as we noted above, Arabic words do not usually end in alif: the usual spelling for final long vowel alif is ى. Therefore, when you see a word that ends in alif (such as شكرا), consider the possibility that the alif represents تنوين الفتح.

Remember that alif at the end of a word probably means one of two things: (a) the word is a proper noun, or (b) the word has the ending تنوين الفتح. Also, the sound *an* at the end of a word usually indicates تنوين الفتح.

In fully vowelled texts, تنوين الفتح is written as a double fatHa when it occurs on ة or final اء. When it occurs on other letters, it is written as an alif with a double fatHa, which can rest either on top of or slightly in front of the alif, depending on the script or font used. Practice writing تنوين الفتح by copying the examples:

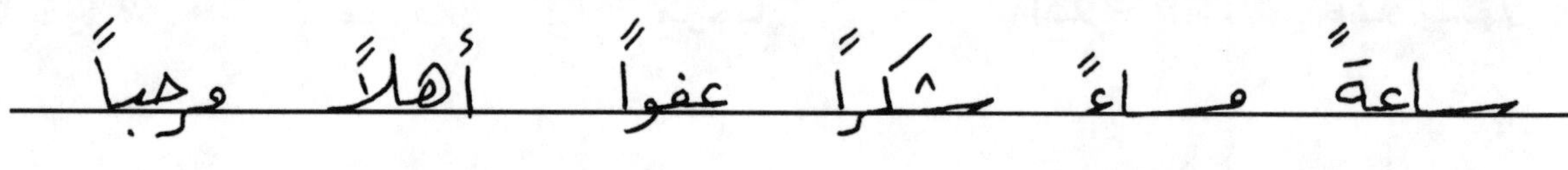

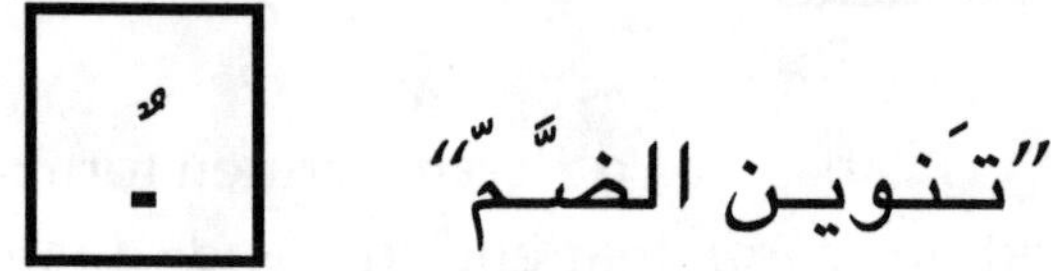

"تَنوين الضَّمّ"

This symbol is called تنوين الضمّ and is pronounced *un*. It represents a certain grammatical ending on indefinite nouns and adjectives. You will see or hear it only in fully vowelled texts and formal speeches.

Listening Exercise 4.

Listen to the following examples of تنوين الضمّ and repeat:

كتابٌ　　　استاذةٌ　　　قلمٌ　　　ساعةٌ　　　طالبٌ

Writing

When تنوين الضم is written, it has two main variants, both of which are commonly used and signify the same sound and meaning. These variants are:

ـٌ a ضمّة with a hooked tail　　　　ـٌ two ضمّة 's

We will not be using تنوين الضم for some time, but you may see or hear it, so learn to recognize these as variants of this grammatical ending. Practice writing it by copying the examples:

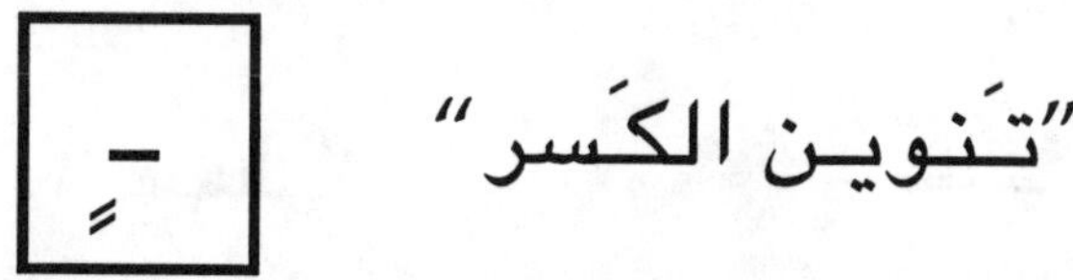

This symbol is called تنوين الكسر and is pronounced *in.* It represents the third and final grammatical ending that can occur on indefinite nouns and adjectives. Like تنوين الضم , it only appears in fully vocalized texts and formal contexts.

Listening Exercise 5.

Listen to the following examples of تنوين الكسر and repeat:

طالبٍ ساعةٍ قلمٍ استاذةٍ كتابٍ

Writing

When it is written in vowelled texts, تنوين الكسر is always written the same way: two kasras. Practice writing it by copying the examples:

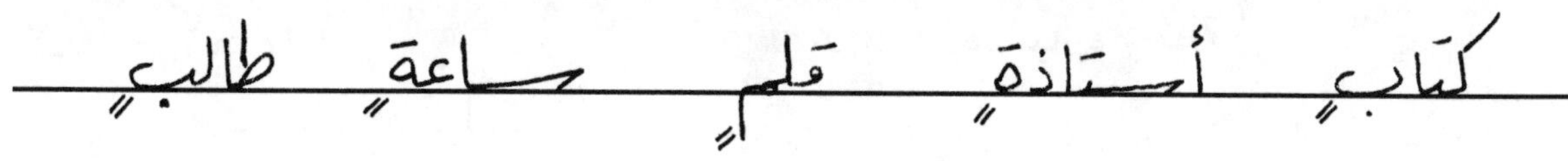

You will learn more about تنوين الضم and تنوين الكسر later, when you begin studying the Quran and classical texts. For now, we will not use them, because they are not used in everyday speech, and informal Arabic does not rely on them to convey meaning. You are only expected to recognize them as "grammatical endings" when you see or hear them.

These three endings, تنوين الفتح , الضم , and الكسر , can occur only on **indefinite** nouns and adjectives. In addition, Arabic has three endings that occur on **definite** nouns and adjectives, which correspond to the three short vowels, فتحة , ضمة , and كسرة . Like the indefinite تنوين endings, these grammatical endings are only used in formal situations and are only written in vocalized texts. Thus, in a formal context, الطالب might be pronounced or marked: الطالبُ or الطالبَ or الطالبِ , depending on the grammatical role of الطالب in the sentence. However, since the grammatical role of the noun in question will be clear from other sentence clues, these endings are usually superfluous to meaning. The important thing for you to remember is that all three of these mean *the student.*

Listening Exercise 6.

Listen to the following words and phrases read with grammatical endings فَتحة , ضَمّة , and كَسرة :

١- الطالبُ   الطالبَ   الطالبِ

٢- الاستاذةُ   الاستاذةَ   الاستاذةِ

٣- مدينةُ نيويورك   مدينةَ نيويورك   مدينةِ نيويورك

You will only see these endings in fully vocalized texts, and only hear them in very formal contexts. We will return to their meanings later; for now, just recognize them as "grammatical endings" when you hear them.

Drill 2.

Read aloud the following phrases, written in formal Arabic and vocalized:

١- – أهلاً وَسَهلاً !
– أهلاً بِك !

٢- – نَعيماً !
– أَنْعَمَ اللّهُ عَلَيْك !

٣- – مَرحَبًا !
– مرحباً بِك !

٤- – شُكراً !
– عَفواً .

٥- الحَمدُ لِلّه !

٦- هِيَ في مدينةِ القاهِرة .

٧- هذا رَجُلٌ طَويل .

٨- هذِهِ سيّارةٌ جميلة .

٩- شاهَدتُ فيلماً فَرَنسيّاً أمس .

١٠- أسْكُن في مَدينةٍ كبيرة .

١١- اِشتَرَيْتُ سيّارةً جديدة .

١٢- اِشتَرى الاستاذُ الكتابَ مِنَ المَكتَبة .

How many of these can you understand? Can you guess any new words from context?

Drill 3.

The following passage is extracted from a children's story written in formal Arabic. Notice that it is fully vowelled, to help school-age children learn the correct pronunciation of words, and also to expose them to the grammatical endings of formal Arabic. First, pick out several examples of Damma, fatHa, and kasra as grammatical endings on definite nouns. Then circle all instances of tanwiin endings.

الكَنز المَدْفُون

كَانَ مَا كَانَ فِي قَدِيمِ الزَّمَانِ، كَانَ فِي إِحْدَى المُدُنِ مَلِكٌ لاَ يُحَقِّقُ لأيِّ إِنْسَانٍ طَلَباً إِلَّا إِذَا حَكَى لَهُ حِكَايَةً مُمْتِعَةً وَمُسَلِّيَةً.

دَخَلَ عَلَيْهِ ذَاتَ يَوْمٍ رَجُلٌ يُرِيْدُ مِنْهُ عَطَاءً، فَقَالَ لَهُ المَلِكُ:

لَا أُعْطِيكَ مَطْلُوبَكَ أَيُّهَا الرَّجُلُ إِلَّا إِذَا قَصَصْتَ لَنَا قِصَّةً نَسْتَأْنِسُ بِهَا.

فَأَجَابَهُ الرَّجُلُ قَائِلاً:

سَمْعاً وَطَاعَةً، ثُمَّ إِنَّهُ تَنَحْنَحَ وَقَالَ:

آعْلَمْ يَا سَيِّدَ آلمُلُوكِ أَنَنَا كُنَّا ثَلَاثَةَ أَخْوَةٍ عِنْدَمَا مَاتَ وَالِدُنَا وَتَرَكَ لَنَا ثَرْوَةً مُؤَلَّفَةً مِنْ ثَلَاثَةِ آلَافِ دِيْنَارٍ،

من قصة "الكنز المسحور"، دار المقاصد للتأليف والطباعة والنشر، بيروت ١٩٩٠

Drill 4.

Circle all occurrences of الـ and the ending ـًا in the following advertisement. Also identify all the words and names you can:

الآن، طيران الخليج توفر لكم ثلاث رحلات اسبوعياً الى فرانكفورت وامستردام كل يوم اثنين وجمعة مروراً بالبحرين، وكل سبت مروراً بالدوحة. المسافرين من السعودية يمكنهم السفر على هذه الرحلات بتحويلات مريحة ومناسبة. تصل هذه الرحلات الى فرانكفورت الساعة ٦,٠٥ صباحاً وامستردام الساعة ٨,١٥ صباحاً.

وسواء اخترت السفر على الدرجة الأولى، أو درجة رجال الاعمال، او الدرجة السياحية، فإنك ستسافر في جو من الراحة والرفاهية حيث تستمتع بكرم ضيافتنا الاصيلة.

كل هذا جزء من تجربة الطيران، بأسلوب طيران الخليج الرفيع.

طيران الخليج

GULF AIR

من جريدة الشرق الاوسط ، ١٩٩٢

Drill 5.

Read the following names of Arab and other Middle Eastern countries aloud, then identify their location on the map and write the number that corresponds to the location of each.

مِصْر ____   الجَزائِر ____   عُمان ____

سوريا ____   العِراق ____   تونِس ____

السّودان ____   الأُردُن ____   لُبنان ____

اليَمَن ____   قَطَر ____   المَغرِب ____

السَّعوديّة ____   الإمارات ____   البَحْرَيْن ____

ليبْيا ____   الكُوَيْت ____   إسْرائيل وفِلَسْطين ____

إيران ____   تُركيّا ____   موريتانيا ____

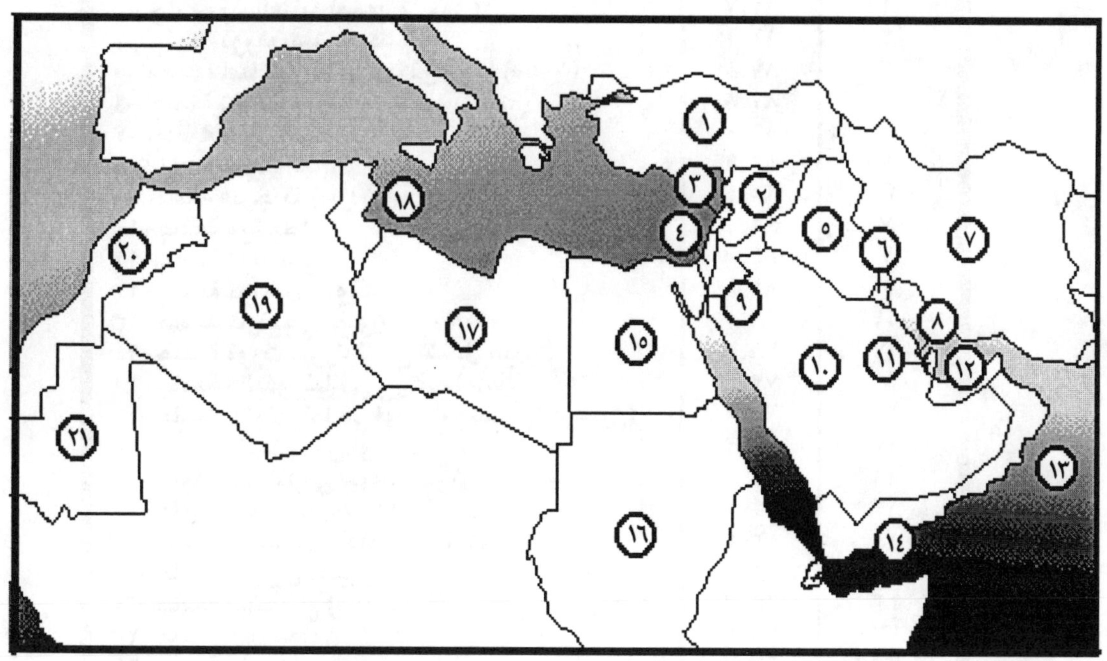

Drill 6.

Following is a list of top business schools.

1. Find out:
   (a) whether your school is listed among them.
   (b) the top three schools.
   (c) the top three schools in your geographical area.

2. To which five schools you would apply if you were thinking of business school?

3. Guess the meaning of:
   (a) كلية _______________
   (b) معهد _______________

افضل كليات التجارة وادارة الاعمال

درجة التصنيف / الجامعة	مجموع النقاط	المكانة العلمية
١- جامعة هارفارد	١٠٠,٠	٢
٢- جامعة ستانفورد	٩٧,٩	١
٣- جامعة بنسلفانيا (معهد وارتون)	٩٢,٧	٢
٤- جامعة نورثويسترن (كيلوج)	٩١,١	٢
٥- معهد ماساتشوستس للتكنولوجيا (سلون)	٨٩,٨	٢
٦- جامعة شيكاجو	٨٧,٨	٦
٧- جامعة ديوك (فوكوا)	٨٦,٠	١١
٨-كلية دارتموث (تك)،	٨٥,٦	٧
٩- جامعة فيرجينا (داردن)	٨٥,٤	١١
١٠-جامعة ميشيجان	٨٥,٢	٧
١١-جامعة كولومبيا	٨٤,٥	٧
١٢-جامعة كورنيل (جونسون)	٨١,١	١١
١٣-جامعة كارنيجي ميلون	٧٨,٥	١١
١٤-جامعة نورث كاورلينا في تشابل هيل	٧٨,٣	١٧
١٥-جامعة كاليفورنيا في بيركلي (هاس)	٧٧,٤	٧
١٦-جامعة كاليفورنيا في لوس أنجليس (اندرسون)	٧٦,٧	١١
١٧-جامعة تكساس في اوستن	٧٦,٢	١٧
١٨-جامعة انديانا في بلومينجتون	٧٦,١	١٦
١٩-جامعة نيويورك (شترن)	٧٤,٦	١٧
٢٠-جامعة بيردو في انديانا (كرانرت)	٧٣,٤	٢٠
٢١-جامعة سوزرن كاليفورنيا	٧١,٧	٢٥
٢٢-جامعة بيتسبرج (كاتس)	٦٨,٧	٣٣
٢٣-جامعة جورجتاون	٦٨,٧	٣٧
٢٤-جامعة ماريلاند في كوليج بارك	٦٧,٧	٣٣
٢٥-جامعة روتشستر (سيمون) في نيويورك	٦٧,٢	٢٢

من مجلة المجلة، أيار (مايو) ١٩٩١

Drill 7.

Read the names of these cars. What do you notice about the spelling of foreign letters and sounds in Arabic?

من جريدة الشرق الاوسط ، ١٩٩٣

Drill 8.

Skim through the following ad and sound out the words. What is being advertised here?

من جريدة الشرق الاوسط، ١٩٩٢

Drill 9.

Find a copy of an Arabic newspaper (there may be one in your university library, or in a foreign bookstore or newsstand). Look for words you recognize, such as names, and write out ten. Hint: good places to look are on the front page for names of people and places in the news, and in advertisements, such as the ones you have seen in previous units.

Culture الثقافة

Video

Watch Scenes 17 and 18 with your teacher.

Visiting

Every culture has its own set of expectations and behaviors involving visiting. In Arab culture, hospitality is a highly prized virtue, and when you visit people at their home or workplace, they will generally insist that you at least have something to drink. The most common items offered are coffee, tea, and soft drinks. If you are invited for a meal, expect lots of food, for the hosts will go out of their way to serve you the most lavish meal they can. They will also keep piling food on your plate and insisting that you eat more! When you have had enough to eat, say الحَمدُ لِلّه .

You noticed in the video scenes that when the hostess first offered a drink, the guest refused. The initial offer and refusal are somewhat formulaic in Arab culture, and are basically expressions of politeness on both sides. The guest refuses at first because he or she does not want to put the host out, and to show that he or she has not come just to have something to drink. A guest will often refuse several times before accepting.

When you are offered something, it is your responsibility as "offeree" not to impose too greatly. The offerer will go out of his or her way to be generous, but that is not an invitation for you to take advantage of the hospitality. Likewise, when you are entertaining, remember to fulfill your role as host by insisting.

الوحدة العاشرة

UNIT TEN

برافو! You have now learned all of the symbols used in writing Arabic. The following chart reviews the letters and their names in modern alphabetical order:

Connector?	Final	Medial	Initial	الاسم	الحرف
×	ـا	ـا	ا	الف	ا
√	ـب	ـبـ	بـ	باء	ب
√	ـت	ـتـ	تـ	تاء	ت
√	ـث	ـثـ	ثـ	ثاء	ث
√	ـج	ـجـ	جـ	جيم	ج
√	ـح	ـحـ	حـ	حاء	ح
√	ـخ	ـخـ	خـ	خاء	خ
×	ـد	ـد	د	دال	د
×	ـذ	ـذ	ذ	ذال	ذ
×	ـر	ـر	ر	راء	ر
×	ـز	ـز	ز	زاي	ز
√	ـس	ـسـ	سـ	سين	س
√	ـش	ـشـ	شـ	شين	ش
√	ـص	ـصـ	صـ	صاد	ص
√	ـض	ـضـ	ضـ	ضاد	ض
√	ـط	ـطـ	طـ	طاء	ط
√	ـظ	ـظـ	ظـ	ظاء	ظ
√	ـع	ـعـ	عـ	عين	ع
√	ـغ	ـغـ	غـ	غين	غ
√	ـف	ـفـ	فـ	فاء	ف
√	ـق	ـقـ	قـ	قاف	ق
√	ـك	ـكـ	كـ	كاف	ك
√	ـل	ـلـ	لـ	لام	ل
√	ـم	ـمـ	مـ	ميم	م
√	ـن	ـنـ	نـ	نون	ن
√	ـه	ـهـ	هـ	هاء	هـ
×	ـو	ـو	و	واو	و
√	ـي	ـيـ	يـ	ياء	ي

This alphabetical order is used in modern dictionaries; you **must** know it to look up words. Start memorizing now, a few letters at a time.

The next chart reviews the extra-alphabetical symbols that you have learned:

الاسم	symbol	الاسم	symbol
وَصلة	ٱ	فَتحة	ـَ
ألِف مَدّة	آ	ضَمّة	ـُ
dagger alif	ـٰ	كَسرة	ـِ
ألِف مَقصورة	ى	سُكون	ـْ
تَنوين الفتح	ـًا	هَمزة	ء
تَنوين الضَمّ	ـٌ	شَدّة	ـّ
تنوين الكسر	ـٍ	تاء مَربوطة	ة

Listening Exercise 1.

Surprise! Listen to the tape.

Drill 1.

Listed below are names of some Arab authors you need to include in a bibliography. Alphabetize them according to the Arabic alphabet. **Disregard الـ** .

غُرَيِّب   الخوري   بساط   عَوَض

مُطران   مُهَنّا   وَهبَه   عَبد الرّازِق

الغانِم   نادِر   العِنداري   جَفّال

صابِر   السَّنهوري   الخَليل   الخالِدي

صَفيّ الدّين   القاسِم   دَرويش   الكَيّالي

الدُّسوقي   القَبّاني   السَّمّان   الشَّيْخ

One-Letter Particles

Particles and prepositions that consist of only one letter are written **connected to the following word.** The most common of these are:

و	*and*
لِـ	*for, belong to* (indicates possession)
بِـ	*by, with* (indicates instrument)
فَـ	*thus, therefore, so*

Remember: لـ , بـ , and فـ are all connecting letters and so are attached to the following word. Since the letter و does not connect, **it must be written close to the following word, and should never be left "stranded" at the end of a line.**

لِلـ <— الـ + لِـ

When the preposition لـ is written with a word beginning with الـ , a spelling rule prescribes that **alif is dropped, and the two** لـ**'s are connected**. For example, to write preposition لـ with noun الطالب , *belonging to the student,* drop the alif of الـ and write preposition لـ connected to the لـ of الطالب like this: للطالب .

Drill 2.

Practice connecting و , لـ , and ب in the following phrases:

(you and I)	________________	١- انا + و + انت
(in English)	________________	٢- بـ + الإنجليزية
(for the doctor)	________________	٣- لـ + الدكتور
(in Arabic)	________________	٤- بـ + العربية
(and you?)	________________	٥- و + حضرتك؟
(for the teacher)	________________	٦- لـ + الأستاذ
(with computers)	________________	٧- بـ + الكمبيوتر
(by car)	________________	٨- بـ + السيارة
(for the girl)	________________	٩- لـ + البنت
(for the boy)	________________	١٠- لـ + الولد

Drill 3.

Not all occurrences of word-initial و , بـ , لـ , or فـ are occurrences of these particles, but many are, and so you should be on the lookout for them. For practice, skim the text and circle all words that look like they begin with لـ , و , بـ , or فـ :

الكمبيوتر العربي
يواكب آخر
تطورات العصر

ويقدم

Microsoft Windows 3.1

بدعم للغة العربية

يدعم كل برامج MS-DOS الشائعة (نافذة،
مساعد العربي، آراب وورد، أي بي إم ان
ال اس، بلال .... الخ)، ويسمح باستخدام
ميزتي القص واللصق بينها، حيث تتم
عملية الترجمة تلقائيا.

يوفر الاحرف المطبعية TrueType
العربية بالاضافة الى جميع رموز التشكيل،
والتغيير تلقائيا في المقاسات لكل
الاحجام على كافة الطابعات التي
يعتمدها Microsoft Windows 3.1.

مزود ببرنامج Write لتنسيق النصوص
المعرب تعريبا كاملا، بالاضافة الى
التطبيقات الاخرى مثل التقويم الذي يعتمد
النظامين الهجري والميلادي.

Microsoft Windows 3.1 بدعم للغة
العربية غير مؤمن ولا يتطلب أية أجهزة أو
برامج أخرى لتشغيله

يبلغ سعر Microsoft Windows 3.1 بدعم
للغة العربية ١٤٩ دولارا فقط ، واذا ابتعت
البرنامج الآن ستصلك النسخة العربية الكاملة
التي ستصدر في نوفمبر مجانا.* واذا
كان لديك حاليا النسخة الانكليزية من
Microsoft Windows 3.1 فبإمكانك تطويرها
الى النسخة العربية مقابل ٧٥ دولارا فقط.

Microsoft Windows 3.1 بدعم للغة العربية
لاتقبل بديلا له

مايكروسوفت

* لاتشمل البريد والتغليف

للحصول على نسختك من Microsoft Windows 3.1 بدعم
للغة العربية، يرجى الاتصال باقرب موزع معتمد او
اكمل هذه القسيمة وارسلها الى :

مايكروسوفت الشرق الاوسط (Microsoft Middle East)
ص. ب: ١٤١٣٥ دبي ـ الإمارات العربية المتحدة

الرجاء إضافة ٢٠ دولار تكاليف الشحن والتغليف،
وعدم إرسال عملات نقدية.

من جريدة الشرق الاوسط ، ١٩٩٢

Justification of Margins

In type or print, margins may be justified or evened by lengthening the connecting segment between letters. This may be done between any two connecting letters; it does not affect the reading of the word at all. For example, الكتاب may be written: الكـــتـاب or الكتـــــاب . **Do not confuse this lengthening, which occurs only in print, with that of toothless ســ (——), which occurs only in handwriting.**

Drill 4.

Circle all examples of margin justification you can find in the following poem:

سَـقفُ بـيتـي حَديـــدْ   رُكــنُ بــيـتـي حَجــرْ

فــاعْـصفـي يـا ريـــاح   وانــــتـحِـبْ يـا شـــجرْ

واسـْبحـــي يـا غـيـــومْ   واهــطِلي بـالـمـــطـرْ

واقــْصفـي يـا رعـــودْ   لــستُ أخـشى خـطَرْ

ســقـفُ بـيـتـي حــديــدْ   رُكــنُ بـيـتـي حــجــرْ

من قصيدة " الطمأنينة " لميخائيل نعيمة

Drill 5.

The following is the solution to an Arabic crossword puzzle. Connect the letters in this puzzle to form words (ignore single letters):

٢٠	١٩	١٨	١٧	١٦	١٥	١٤	١٣	١٢	١١	١٠	٩	٨	٧	٦	٥	٤	٣	٢	١	
ا	■	ن	و	ف	ز	ع	ي	■	ن	ا	ط	ر	س	ل	ا	ر	ا	د	م	١
ل	■	ب	ا	ق	ر	■	د	ي	ج	ت	■	ن	ي	ج	و	ر	ت	ي	ن	٢
ح	ا	ر	■	ط	ي	ق	ل	■	ي	و	ا	ت	ف	■	ا	■	ي	ن	غ	٣
ب	ن	ر	ا	■	أ	ر	■	ه	ر	ا	س	ج	■	ا	ن	ا	■	ا	و	٤
ر	ي	■	ل	ا	ب	ي	ن	ا	ه	■	ت	ن	ا	ل	■	ق	ي	ص	ل	٥
■	ن	ي	م	س	■	ه	ي	م	ا	ك	ر	■	ب	ا	■	ف	س	و	ي	٦
ه	■	ح	ي	ت	ا	■	ا	ب	■	ر	ا	■	ر	ي	ش	ا	د	ر	ا	٧

Horizontal

-١ ________ ________ (two words) ________ ،

-٢ ________ ، ________ ، ________

-٣ ________ ، ________ ، ________ ، ________

-٤ ________ ، ________ ، ________ ، ________ ، ________

-٥ ________ ، ________ ، ________ ، ________

-٦ ________ ، ________ ، ________ ، ________

-٧ ________ ، ________ ، ________ ، ________

Vertical

-١ ________

-٢ ________

-٣ ________ ، ________

-٤ ________ ، ________

-٥ ________

-٦ ________ ، ________

-٧ ________ ، ________

-٨ ________

-٩ ________

-١٠ ________ ، ________

-١١ ________

-١٢ ________

-١٣ ________ ، ________

-١٤ ________

-١٥ ________

-١٦ ________ ، ________

-١٧ ________ ، ________

-١٨ ________ ، ________

-١٩ ________

-٢٠ ________

Drill 6.

Read and learn the following expressions that we will be using in class:

homework	واجِب
drill	تَمْرين
lesson	دَرس
text	نَصّ
page	صَفْحة
word	كَلِمة

I have a question	عندي سُؤال
	يا استاذ! عندي سؤال.
I did not understand	ما فَهِمْت
	ما فهمت هذه الكلمة!
I don't know	لا أعرِف
	لا أعرف هذه الكلمة .
How do we say..?	كَيف نَقول ...؟
	كيف نقول "I forgot" بالعربية؟
Thank you—You're welcome	شُكرًا — عَفوًا
Please	مِن فَضلِك
A second time, once more (to request repetition)	مرّة ثانية ، من فضلك!

Handwriting

As you have been learning throughout this workbook, Arabic handwriting exhibits some variations from the printed form. In addition, handwriting itself varies according to individual style. With practice, you will gradually learn to recognize various handwriting styles and conventions.

Drill 7.

Read as much as you can of the following handwriting samples. Look for familiar words and try to guess new ones from context. What observations can you make about the variation of letters in handwriting styles? After reading, write a similar passage providing information about yourself.

Sample I:

اهلا وسهلا !
اسمي غادة عبد الكريم وانا من مدينة حلب
في سوريا وبيتي في شارع الجلاء.
انا استاذة في جامعة حلب.

Sample II:

اهلاً وسهلاً !
اسمي عبد الحميد بومداس وانا من مدينة
طرابلس في ليبيا وبيتي في شارع الثورة.
انا طالب في جامعة طرابلس.

Sample III:

اهلا وسهلا !
إسمى سيف الله عبد النور وأنا من مدينة
المنصورة فى مصر وبيتى فى شارع جمال عبد
الناصر.. أنا أستاذ فى جامعة المنصورة.

Culture الثقافة

Development of the Arabic Writing System

The Arabic writing system is believed to have evolved from the Aramaic script through the Nabateans, Arab tribes living to the north of the Arabian Peninsula (present-day Jordan) in pre-Islamic times. This early version of Arabic script survives in inscriptions dating back to the third and fourth centuries A.D., which represent the earliest known of many stages of development. Although writing was known in the Arabian Peninsula before Islam, it was the early Muslims who developed the script that we know today, in order to preserve the text of the Quran by putting it down in writing. Tradition holds that the first compilation of the Quran was recorded during the reign of Uthman (عُـثـمـان), the third Caliph (d. A.D. 656). Even then, though, the script was not complete, for surviving fragments show text devoid of short vowel markings and dots, as the following sample shows:[1]

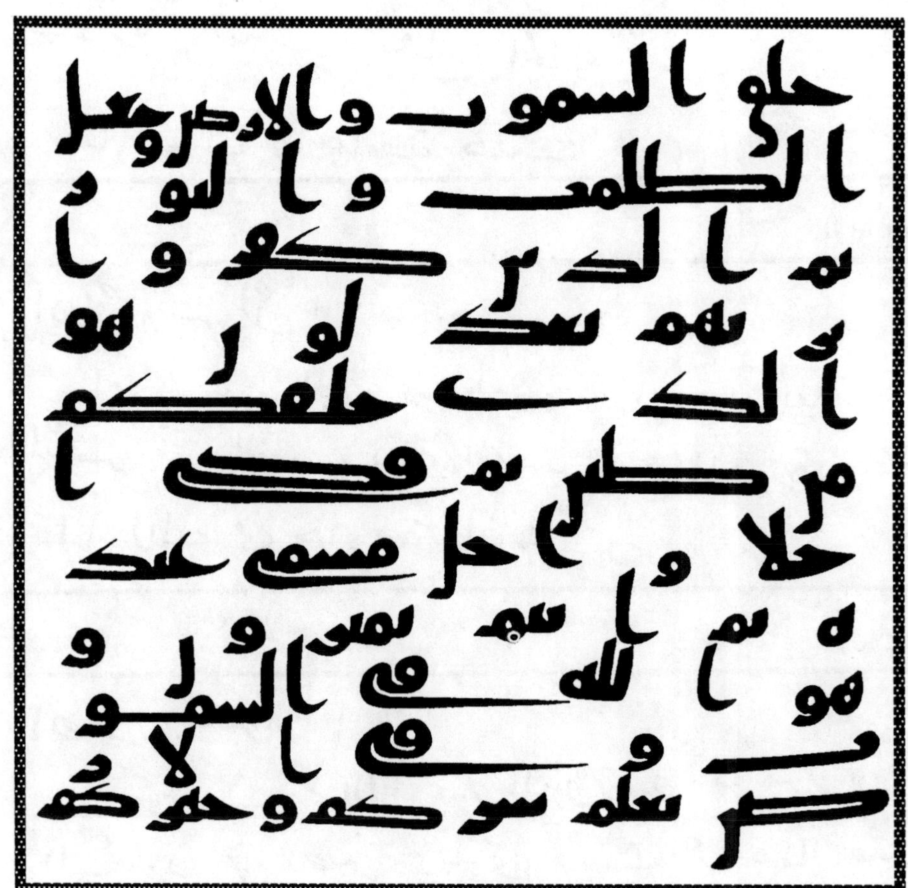

[1]The examples in this section are taken from روح الخط العربي، تأليف كامل البابا، دار العلم للملايين، بيروت ١٩٨٨ .

The addition of short vowel markings began during the reign of Ali (علي), the fourth Caliph (d. A.D. 661), and the dots that distinguish between letters of similar shape were added during Umayyad rule, around the end of the seventh century. Further development of the individual shapes of letters occurred at the beginning of the Abbasid period (from A.D. 750).

Calligraphy

Calligraphy is a highly developed art form. Since the time of the earliest script form you saw above, called Kufic, artists have continuously developed new styles and designs. Quranic verses, poetry, and proverbs written in intricate scripts often adorn books, monuments, and public buildings. Professional calligraphers combine form and meaning by working Quranic verses into pictures such that the letters and dots form a design. Below are four artistic renderings of the phrase

(*In the Name of God the Merciful and Compassionate*) بِسم الله الرَحمن الرَحيم

See how many letters you can pick out in each sample:

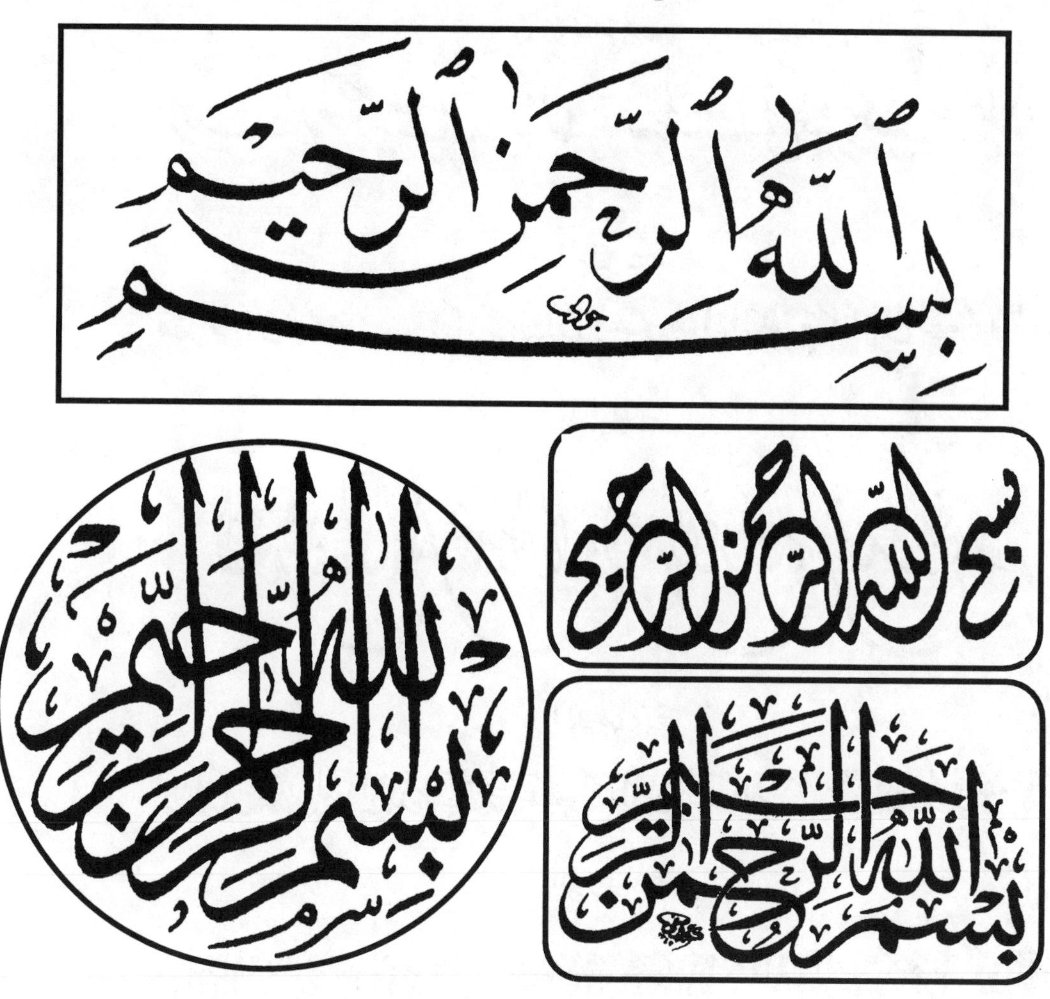

Following are names and examples of well-known calligraphic scripts:

الكوفي

ربنا آتنا في الدنيا حسنة وفي الآخرة حسنة وقنا عذاب النار

النسخي

لا تنتظر أن تسنح لك فرص خارقة للعادة بل انتهز الفرص العادية واجعلها عظيمة

الثلث

لا وسادة أنعم من صدر الأم ولا وردة أجمل من ثغرها

الفارسي

رب يوم بكيت منه فلما صرت في غيره بكيت عليه

الرقعي

خير للمرء أن يموت في سبيل فكرته من أن يعيش طول الدهر جبانا عن نصرة وطنه

الديواني

اعمل لدنياك كأنك تعيش أبدا واعمل لآخرتك كأنك تموت غدا

الإجازة

إذا أقبل البخت باضت الدجاجة على عمود وإذا أدبر البخت انشق الهاون في الشمس

الديواني الجلي

رب أوزعني أن أشكر نعمتك التي أنعمت علي وعلى والدي وأن أعمل صالحا ترضاه وأدخلني برحمتك في عبادك الصالحين

Drill 8.

Following are advertisements in different script styles. Copy them out in your own handwriting:

1.

2.

3.

4.

5.

6.

7. البنك العربي

8. بنك القاهرة السعودي

9. مشروع الرَّي والصرف
بالاحساء

10. 

★ تمّ بحمد الله ★

APPENDIX

نصوص الحوارات بالعامية المصرية المسجلة على شريط الڤيديو المصاحب للكتاب

TEXTS OF THE EGYPTIAN COLLOQUIAL DIALOGUES ON THE ACCOMPANYING VIDEO TAPE

المشهد الأول Scene One

أهلاً !

- أهْلاً !

+ أهلاً بيك .

- اِسْمي أحْمد واسم حَضْرِتِك ؟

+ اِسمي نيللي .

- تَشَرّفْنا .

+ تشرّفنا بيك .

المشهد الثاني Scene Two

اسمي محمود

أهلاً وسَهْلاً .. اِسمي مَحْمود البَطَل ، أنا مِن مَدينة بَيْروت في لُبنان .

المشهد الثالث Scene Three

حضرتك من مصر ؟

- أهلاً وسهلاً .

+ أهلاً وسهلاً بيك .

- اِسمي خالِد ، واسم حضرتِك ؟

+ اِسمي سامية .

- تشرّفنا ... حضرتِك من مَصْر ؟

+ أَيْوه من مصر .

- أهلاً وسهلاً .

+ أهلاً بيك ، وحضرتَك ؟

- أنا من اسْكِنْدِرِيّة .

+ أهلاً وسهلاً .

- أهلاً بيكِ .

المشهد الرابع Scene Four

صباح الخير

- صَباح الخير يا دُكْتور عبّاس .

+ أهلاً .. صباح النّور يا دكتور أحمد .. إزَّيّك ؟

- الحَمْدُ لِله ، وازيّك انْتَ ؟

+ الحمد لله ، وإزّي المَدام ؟

- كوَيِّسة ، الحمد للّه .

+ الحمد للّه .

المشهد الخامس Scene Five

مساء الخير

- مَساء الخير يا لَمْيا .

+ مساء الخير يا مدام هُدى .. اِتْفَضّلي .

وازَّي حضرتِك ؟

- الحمد للّه ... إزّيِك انتِ ؟

+ الحمد لله .. وازَّي الدُّكتور أمين ؟

- كويّس ، الحمد لله .

المشهد السادس Scene Six

إزيّك ؟

- أهلاً يادكتور أحمد .

+ أهلاً يا علي .. اتفضَّل .

- أهلاً يادكتور أحمد .. إزَّيّك ؟

- الحمد لله ، وازّيك إنتَ ؟

+ الحمد لله ... اِبْراهيم صاحْبي .. طالِب في جامعة القاهِرة .

- تشرَّفنا .

× تشرَّفنا بيك .

المشهد السابع SCENE SEVEN

الحمد للّـه !

- أهلاً وسهلاً .

+ أهلاً ياسامية.

- إزّيك يا لَميا ؟

- الحمد لله .

- أهلاً .

× أهلاً وسهلاً بيكِ .

- اتفضّلوا ... أهلاً وسهلاً .

+ أهلاً بيكِ .

- إزّيِّك ؟

+ الحمد لله .. إزّيِّك انتِ ؟

+ الحمد لله .. سامية صاحبِتي ... طالبة في جامعة اسكِنْدرِيّة .

- أهلاً وسهلاً .

× أهلاً وسهلاً بيكِ .

المشهد الثامن SCENE EIGHT

تشرّفنا !

- مساء الخير يا دكتور عبّاس .

+ مساء النور يا دكتورمحمود .. إزّيّـك ؟

- الحمد لله .. إزيك انتَ ؟

+ الحمد لله .

- الدُّكتور أحمد سَلامة ... الدكتور محمود البطل .

× أهلاً وسهلاً .

- أهلاً وسهلاً بيك .. تشرّفنا .

× تشرّفنا بيك .

+ اتفضّـل يا دكتور .

+ شكراً .. شكراً .

× حضرتك استاذ في الجامعة الأمْريكيّـة ؟

+ لا ..في الحقيقة أنا أستاذ في جامعة إيموري في مدينة أطْلانْطا في أمريكا .

× أهلاً وسهلاً .. تشرفنا.

+ أهلاً وسهلاً بيك .. وحضرتَك ؟

× أنا أستاذ في جامعة القاهرة .

+ أهلاً وسهلاً .

× أهلاً بيك .

+ أهلاً .

المشهد التاسع SCENE NINE

مَع السّلامة !

... يَللا ياولاد .. مَعَ أَلْف سَلامة .. رَبِّنا مَعاك !

× مَعَ السَّلامة ياجابِر !

× مَعَ السَّلامة ياجابِر .

.. مع السّلامة !

من فيلم " اِحْنا بتوع الاوتوبيس "

المشهد العاشر SCENE TEN

انتِ رايحة فين ؟

– صباح الخير يا لَمْيا .

+ صباح النّور يا سامية .

– إنتِ رايحة فين ؟

+ عندي فَصْل .

– طَيِّب .. اتفضَّلي ، مع السّلامة .

+ الله يسَلِّمِك .

المشهد الحادي عشر SCENE ELEVEN

طيّب ، اتفضّلي !

– مساء الخير يا ليا .

+ مساء النور يا دكتور .

– إزيّك ؟

+ الحمد لله .. وازّي حضرتَك ؟

– الحمد لله .

+ وازي الدُّكتورة ؟

– كويّسة .. الحمد لله .

+ طَب عَن إِذْنَك .. عندي فَصْل .

– طَيّب .. اتفضّلي .

المشهد الثاني عشر SCENE TWELVE

انتَ ساكن فين ؟

– مساء الخير ... مساء الخير ياعباس .

+ مساء النور يا عَبْد الحَكيم ... إزّيك ؟

– الحمد لله .. إزّيك إنتَ ؟

+ كويس .. الحمد للّه .

– تِشْرب قهوة ؟

+ فين ؟

– هنا .. في البيت عندي .

+ إنت ساكِن فين ؟

– في شارع مُراد .

+ واللّهِ !! ... طيب يَلا بينا .

– يللا بينا .

المشهد الثالث عشر SCENE THIRTEEN

اسم الكريم إيه ؟

- أهلاً .. أهلاً .. تَحْت أَمْرَك ياشيخ ... إسم الكَريم إيه ؟

+ عِبيد .

- تشرّفنا يا شيخ عبيد .. أنا اسمي حُسْني .

+ أهلاً .. أهلاً .

- إنتَ رايِح فين ؟

+ رايح شارِع مُراد .

- شارع مراد .. شارع مراد .. أيوه ، يبقى من هنا .. أيوه ، تَعالَ أَوَصّلَك .

+ جَزاك الله كُل خير ياأستاذ حسني .

- العَفْو يا شيخ عبيد .. على إيه ياراجِل ؟!.. كُلِّنا إخْوة .

من فيلم " الكيت كات "

المشهد الرابع عشر SCENE FOURTEEN

آلو !

- آلو

+ آلو .. حضرتِك الدكتورة زَيْنَب طه ؟

- لا .. النِّمْرة غَلَط .

+ آه ، طب آسفة .

- مَعْليشّ .

المشهد الخامس عشر SCENE FIFTEEN

السلام عليكم

- السَّلامُ عَلَيْكُم .

+ وَعَلَيْكُمُ السَّلام .

- مِن فَضْلَك ، مَكْتَب الدكتور عادِل مُصْطفى فين ؟

+ الباب دا .. تالِت مكتب على اليمِين .

- شكراً .

+ عَفْواً .

المشهد السادس عشر Scene Sixteen

سينما ريڤولي فين ؟

- من فضلَك !

+ أيوه .

- سينما ريڤولي فين ؟

+ أُدخُل يِمين وبَعْدين أَوِّل شِمال علَى طول .

- شُكراً .

+ بالسَّلامة .

المشهد السابع عشر Scene Seventeen

لازم تشربي حاجة

- مساء الخير يا مدام هدى .

+ مساء النور .. أهلاً وسهلاً .. اتفضَّلي .

- شكراً ...

- إزَّي حضرتِك ؟

+ الحمد لله .. إزَّيِّك انتِ ؟

- الحمد لله .

+ تِشْرَبي إيه ؟

- لا .. وَلا حاجة .

+ لا ... لازِم تشربي حاجة .

- واللّه ولا حاجة .

+ شاي وَلاّ قهْوة ؟

- طيِّب ... شاي .

المشهد الثامن عشر SCENE EIGHTEEN

لا ... ولا حاجة !

- مساء الخير يا مدام هدى .

+ مساء النور يا دكتور عَبْد الحَكيم .. أهلاً وسهلاً .

- أهلاً بيكِ يا افَنْدِم .

+ إتفضَّل .

- شكراً يا افندم .

و ازَّي حضرتِك ؟

+ الحمد لله .. إزيَّك إنتَ ؟

- الحمد لله .

+ وازَّي المدام ؟

- كويّسة ، الحمد لله .

+ تِشْرَب قهوة ؟

- لا .. لا .. شكراً .

+ تشرب إيه ؟

- لا .. لا .. ولا حاجة .

+ لا !.. لازم تشرب حاجة .

- طيّب ، قهوة .

× اتفضَّل .

- شكراً .

× اتفضَّلي .

+ شكراً .

قاموس إنجليزي- عربي

English-Arabic Glossary

A

address	عُنْوان
airplane	طائِرة
and	وَ
angry	غَضْبان / غَضبانة
Arab, Arabic	عَرَبي /عَرَبيّة

B

beautiful	جَميل/ جَميلة
behind	وَراء
big	كَبير / كَبيرة
book	كِتاب
bookstore	مَكْتَبة
boy	وَلَد
bread	خُبْز
pita bread	خُبْز عَرَبي
building	بِناية
bus	أوتوبيس
but	لٰكِن

C

car	سَيّارة
cassette tape	شَريط
chair	كُرسي
city	مَدينة
class / classroom	فَصْل ؛ صَفّ

clock / watch	ساعة
close	قَريب / قَريبة
coffee	قَهْوة
Arabic coffee	قَهْوة عَرَبيّة
American coffee	قَهْوة أمْريكيّة
cold (a cold)	بَرْد
cold (feeling cold)	بَرْدان / بَرْدانة

D

difficult / hard	صَعْب
door	باب
doctor (M.D., Ph.D.)	دُكْتور / دُكْتورة
drill	تَمْرين

E

easy	سَهْل / سَهْلة
Egypt	مِصْر
examination / test	اِمْتِحان
excuse me	عَن إذنِك — تفَضّل / تفَضّلي (reply)
exercise	تَمْرين
evening	مَساء

F

far	بَعيد / بَعيدة
fine / good	كويِّس / كويِّسة
friend	صاحِب / صاحِبة
from	مِن

girl	بِنْت
God	اللّه
expression used when praising someone	ما شاءَ اللّه !
God willing	إنْ شاءَ اللّه
in the name of God	بِسْمِ اللّه
may God have mercy on him	اللّه يِرْحَمُه
there is no god but God	لا إله إلاّ اللّه
good / fine	جَيِّد / جَيِّدة ؛ كويِّس / كويِّسة
good hearted (for people) / tasty (for food)	طَيِّب / طَيِّبة
good evening	مَساء الخَير — مَساء النّور (reply)
good morning	صَباح الخَير — صَباح النّور (reply)
good bye	مَعَ السّلامة — اللّه يسَلّمك (reply)

H

hard / difficult	صَعْب / صَعْبة
have: I have	عِنْدي
he	هُوَ
headache	صُداع
hello	أهْلاً (وَسَهْلاً) — أهْلاً بِك (reply)
	السّلامُ عَلَيْكُم — وَعَلَيْكُمُ السّلام (reply)
	مَرحَبًا — أهْلاً / مَرْحبتَيْن (reply)
homework	واجِب
hot (feeling hot)	حَرّان / حَرّانة
house / home	بَيْت

how ?	كَيْفَ ؟
how are you?	ازَّيك ؟ / كَيْفَ الحال ؟
hungry	جَوْعان / جَوْعانة

I

I	أنا
in	في
in front of	أمام

K

know: I know	أعْرِف
I don't know	لا أعْرِف

L

lesson	دَرْس
library / bookstore	مَكْتَبة

M

madam	مَدام
man	رَجُلْ
milk	حَليب (لَبَن)
miss	آنِسة
Mr.	سَيِّد
Mrs.	سَيِّدة / مَدام
money	فُلوس
morning	صَباح

N

name	اِسْم
never mind , that's OK	مَعْلِهش (مَعْليش)
new	جَديد / جَديدة
no	لا
notebook	دَفْتَر
numbers	أرْقام
zero	صِفِر (٠)
one	واحِد (١)
two	اِثنان (٢)
three	ثَلاثة (٣)
four	أرْبَعة (٤)
five	خَمْسة (٥)
six	سِتّة (٦)
seven	سَبْعة (٧)
eight	ثَمانِية (٨)
nine	تِسْعة (٩)
ten	عَشَرة (١٠)

O

office	مَكْتَب
old	قَديم / قَديمة

P

page	صَفْحة
paper	وَرَقة

pen / pencil	قَلَم
please	مِنْ فَضْلِك
please (come in / go ahead / sit down)	تفَضَّل / تفَضَّلي
professor	أُستاذ / أُستاذة

Q

question	سُؤال

R

room	غُرْفة

S

sad , upset	زَعْلان / زَعْلانة
say: we say	نَقول
how do we say ?	كَيْفَ نَقول ؟
she	هِيَ
short	قَصير / قَصيرة
sick	مَريض / مَريضة
small	صَغير / صَغيرة
spacious / wide	واسِع / واسِعة
street	شارِع
student	طالِب / طالِبة
sugar	سُكَّر

T

table	طاوِلة
tall	طَويل / طَويلة

tape (audio, video)	شَريط
tea	شاي
teacher	أُسْتاذ / أُسْتاذة
telephone	تليفون
test / examination	اِمْتِحان
text	نَصّ
thank you	شُكْرًا — عَفْوًا (reply)
thanks be to God	الحَمْدُ لِلّه
thirsty	عَطْشان / عَطْشانة
this	هذا / هذِهِ
tired	تَعْبان / تَعْبانة

U

understand: I understood	فَهِمْتُ
I didn't understand	ما فَهِمْتُ

W

watch / clock	ساعة
water	ماء
welcome	أهْلاً وَسَهْلاً — أهْلاً وَسَهْلاً بك (reply)
wide / spacious	واسِع / واسِعة
window	شُبّاك
with	مَع
woman	اِمْرَأة
word	كَلِمة

yes	نَعَمْ / أيْوه
you	أنْتَ / أنْتِ
you (polite)	حَضْرتَك